DYNAMIC AGEING
Ray Hawkins

31 Daily Devotional Meditations
Outlining
The Bible's insights
For a full, satisfying and purposeful life
As we walk down the years
With the Lord

About Ray Hawkins

Ray Hawkins, was born in Sydney Australia into a working class family. Being sent to Sunday School at the Churches of Christ, Rockdale he learnt about his need for the Saviour. It was around the time of the 1959 Sydney Billy Graham Crusade Ray re-affirmed his faith in Jesus Christ. This changed the whole direction of his life.

Ray went to the Australian Churches of Christ (NSW) Bible College and in the final year two special things happened. He was elected Student President and met his future wife, Mary. (She became a multi-published author).

Together they were involved in establishing two new churches in New South Wales and one in Tasmania. They also helped keep one in Queensland from closing. In their senior years they went on three short term mission trips to Africa. After retiring from the Churches of Christ ministry Ray and Mary had a two year ministry in England.

Ray has been Conference President of New South Wales (Australia) Churches of Christ, twice and President of the NSW Churches of Christ Ministers' Association. In Rotary he was President of the Tenambit/Morpeth club and received the 'Paul Harris Fellow' award. Ray is the incoming president of the Probus club in Beauty Point, Tasmania.

Mary and Ray have three children and six grand-children.

He loves preaching and teaching about issues highlighted in the Bible. This led him to write the themed 31 Day Devotional series. These include topics such as: Children, Marriage, The Cross, Christmas and Happiness.

Blog site. http://rayhawkinsauthor.blogspot.com.au

Ray Hawkins.

Dynamic Ageing
Published by Even Before Publishing;
a division of Wombat Books
P. O. Box 1519, Capalaba Qld 4157
www.evenbeforepublishing.com
www.wombatbooks.com.au

© Ray Hawkins 2014
Design and layout by Even Before Publishing

ISBN: 978-1-921632-22-8

National Library of Australia Cataloguing-in-Publication entry
Author: Hawkins, Ray, author.
Title: Dynamic ageing / Ray Hawkins.
ISBN: 9781921632228 (paperback)
Subjects: Aging--Religious aspects.
          Aging--Biblical teaching.
          Older people--Biblical teaching.
          Christian education of older people.
Dewey Number: 204.0846

All rights reserved. No part of this publication may be reproduced, stored in, or introduced into a retreival system, or transmitted, in any form, or by any means (electronic, mechanical, photocopying, recording or otherwise) without the prior written permission of the publisher.

Unless otherwise cited, Scripture quotations are taken from the NRSV Reference bible with the apocrypha. Copyright © 1993 by Zondervan Publishing house. All rights reserved.

Contents

About Ray Hawkins	*1*

Introduction

Too Old — Never!

No Use by Date
Day 1	*11*

When One Hundred Years is Young
Day 2	*13*

A Fruitful Life
Day 3	*15*

God's Self Assessment Chart
Day 4	*17*

An Invitation Too Good to Miss
Day 5	*19*

The Beauty of Grey Hair
Day 6	*21*

Caleb
Day 7	*23*

The Strength of Years
Day 8	*25*

Don't Chase the Wind
Day 9	*27*

Taming the Lions
Day 10	*29*

Making Sure everything is in Order
Day 11	*31*

Give Thanks for the Rooster
Day 12   *33*

God Rules from the Shadows
Day 13   *35*

Key Words for the Ageing — #1: Inheritance
Day 14   *37*

Courageous Ageing
Day 15   *39*

The Testimony of the Walking Stick
Day 16   *41*

Personal Eucharist
Day 17   *43*

Key Words for the Ageing — #2: Years restored
Day 18   *45*

Leave the Baggage Behind
Day 19   *47*

Make their Rising Worthwhile
Day 20   *49*

Medicine for a Heavy Heart
Day 21   *51*

Escapees from the Old Age Prison
Day 22   *53*

Where Dynamic Ageing Begins
Day 23   *55*

Songs in the Night
Day 24   *57*

Be a Spiritual (Grand) Mother
Day 25   *59*

Total Dynamic Ageing
Day 26   *61*

Keeping the Spiritual Weeds under Control
Day 27   *63*

The Dreamtime Cometh
Day 28   *65*

Walking by your Heart
Day 29   *67*

The Might of Widows
Day 30   *69*

It's Departure Time
Day 31   *71*

Mirror on the Wall

Insights to Share

Introduction

Youth may have the spotlight in our society; however in God's kingdom the aged have a special place. Check out the ages of some of the leading figures within Scripture. Despite their many and varied faults and failures these men and women are an inspiration to us.

The enthusiasm of youth is touted as a primary requirement for revitalising the Church. This kind of fervour is good, but the Church will evaporate unless it is nurtured, protected and refreshed by the wisdom, example and faithfulness of the ageing. A 'Timothy' needs a father figure such as a 'Paul'. People facing enemies who oppose God's promises need a 'Caleb'.

Statistically most people make a commitment to Jesus Christ in their youth. This is wonderful. Then their salvation has to undergo degrees of testing and wilderness experiences. As they come through such trials their earlier commitment rings true. Scars may be on their souls but this gives them the benefit of experience. Lessons are learnt which can be passed on.

The following devotional meditations are meant to be an encouragement to know Christ Jesus in and through the ageing process. No one is ever too old, too weak or too indisposed to enjoy the blessing of the Lord. Nor are they outside His scope for significant ministry.

Various groups have their specific mottos. Maybe we who are Christ's ageing disciples might like to consider the following one. We are 'ageing dynamically!'

Ray (ageing dynamically) Hawkins

Too Old — Never!

Too old! Too old? Too old, you say?

Too old for what?

Too old to show love for one another?

Too old to give care to those in bother?

Too old to offer Christ's 'cup of water'?

Too old — never!

Too old! Too old? Too old to pray?

Too old for that?

Too old to ask God to bless me and you?

Too old to thank Him for His word so true?

Too old to bow and seek to be renewed?

Too old — never!

Too old! Too old? Too old to appreciate?

Too old for fun?

Too old to feel the burdens of life?

Too old to cry for those in strife?

Too old to smile at absurdity?

Too old — never!

Too old! Too old? Too old to meditate?

Too old for God?

Too old to honour my Lord and King?

Ray Hawkins

Too old to worship, His praises sing?

Too old to present my offering?

Too old — never!

Too old! Too old? Too old for pleasure?

Too old for praise?

Too old to taste and share in His grace?

Too old to begin to run His race?

Too old to long to behold His face?

Too old — never!

© Raymond N. Hawkins

No Use by Date
Day 1

Reading: Ps 71

Use by dates often appear on food packaging. They are there to tell the customer when the product will lose its freshness and vitality. It also alerts us to the dangers of consuming it after the use by date. Within the business world the same mindset often applies concerning employment. However, the difference is that workers don't have to wear a tag to remind everyone how old they are.

Fortunately, for those in the Kingdom of God there is no such attitude. With the Bible as our guide, the older we are in the things of Christ the more we have to offer. Consider such men as Noah, Abraham, Moses and Daniel. Whether we come into the Kingdom at a young age or in our mature years we increase in value.

I was a chaplain to a retirement village for eighteen years. The difference in the vibrancy, outlook and hope between people of faith and those without was almost tangible. Those whose value was once in their work or status found their present circumstances depressing. Those with a strong confidence in Jesus as their Saviour and Lord knew their worth. It flowed from Him.

Psalm 71 is the account of a man facing, not only age with its issues, but also bitter citizens. Verse 4: 'Rescue me, O my God, from the hand of the wicked, from the grasp of the unjust and cruel.' Verses 10-11: 'My enemies speak concerning me, and those who watch for my life consult together. They say, "pursue and seize that person whom God has forsaken, for there in no one to deliver".'

As he wrestled with this, probably with age related weaknesses, the psalmist draws upon the faithfulness of God from his yesteryears. Verses 19b-21: 'You who have done great things, O God, who is like you? You who have made me see many troubles and calamities will revive me again; from the depths of the earth you will bring me up again. You will increase my honour, and comfort me once again. I will also praise you with the harp for your faithfulness, O my God.'

Such confidence in God's unchanging attitude to us personally creates an atmosphere of trust and hope in the heart. We may not realise it, but an inner fragrance permeates us wherever we are. This fragrance remains true whatever circumstances we face. How is that possible? Because of our faith in Christ Jesus as our Lord and Saviour. This allows His presence within us to be known to others.

Life's situations leave their marks upon us in varying ways. Some will leave this earth with a reasonable degree of health, others through much pain. If it is easier for the healthy to accept the idea of being of use to the Lord, what about the bed ridden? Having sat with people like this I know, even in their weakness and pain, I've seen the beauty of faith. A life enriched by an abiding hope shines through. 2 Corinthians 4:16-18: 'So we do not lose heart. Even though our outer nature is wasting away, our inner nature is being renewed day by day. For this slight momentary affliction is preparing us for an eternal weight of glory beyond all measure, because we look not at what can be seen but at what cannot be seen; for what can be seen is temporary, but what cannot be seen is eternal.'

Ageless: The Lord doesn't have such things as spiritual retirement villages for His aged or infirm disciples. The sphere of these believers may shrink to the size of a bed. The person, however, is still on active duty as God's child and witness!

Rejoice in having no use by date in the Lord's Kingdom!

When One Hundred Years is Young
Day 2

Reading: Isaiah 65:17-25

To reach one hundred years of age was once considered a great milestone, so much so it warranted a letter of congratulations from the reigning British monarch. With improvements in health care and living conditions more people are entering the 'congratulation list'. However, no matter how healthy an individual is there isn't much vim and vigour associated with an age like one hundred.

I've read reports on the human condition which suggests humanity has the capacity to live much longer. There is a reason why this doesn't happen. The Bible presents that reason as the effects of Adam and Eve's act of treason against God. Death and decay entered the world and impacted us all. The toxic fallout from disobedience was to cut short the potential for much longer living. Instead of living well into the hundreds, according to Genesis 5, living to seventy or eighty became an achievement (Psalm 90:10).

One day death will be a stranger. Yes it will be present, but its virulent power will be drastically restricted. Isaiah 65:20: 'No more shall there be in it (Jerusalem) an infant that lives but a few days, or an old person who does not live out a lifetime; for one who dies at a hundred years will be considered a youth, and one who falls short of a hundred will be considered accursed.'

When will that time happen?

We know not the date. However, the scene is written about in a number of Bible books. In fact, when we say the Lord's Prayer we are longing for it. Remember that part where we say 'Your kingdom come on earth ...' that's the time the writers point towards. A lot of events mentioned leading up to this time are yet to happen, but they will!

The centre, indeed the crux, of this fulfilment is Jerusalem. Zechariah 8:2-5: 'Thus says the Lord God of Hosts: I am jealous for Zion with great jealousy

... I will return to Zion, and will dwell in the midst of Jerusalem; Jerusalem shall be called the faithful city, and the mountain of the Lord of Hosts shall be called the holy mountain ... Old men and old women shall again sit in the streets of Jerusalem, each with staff in hand because of their great age. And the streets of the city shall be full of boys and girls playing in its streets.'

Did you notice the two age groups most susceptible to death? They will live free of its terror. Isaiah 11:8-9: 'The nursing child shall play over the hole of the asp, and the weaned child shall put its hand on the adder's den. They will not hurt or destroy on all my holy mountain; for the earth will be full of the knowledge of the Lord as the waters cover the sea.' Those scriptures and others associated with them portray the Lord Jesus' intention. Age really will be dynamic at that time and not limited just for the young!

How will this be? Because Jesus Christ will fulfil His promise to return to earth to judge and to reign from Jerusalem. Those on earth when this happens will experience what is called the Millennium kingdom. That is Christ's one thousand year rule! For us today we will know a far different scenario. According to 1 Thessalonians 4:13-18 we who have made Christ Jesus our Lord and Saviour will meet Him in the air! This will happen when He gives the command. When that takes place, in the twinkling of an eye, we will be transformed. We will see Him! We will be like Him! (1 John 3:1-3). We will be ageless!

Ageless: Revelation 20:6: 'Blessed and holy are those who share in the first resurrection. Over these the second death has no power, but they will be priests of God, and they will reign with him a thousand years.'

A Fruitful Life
Day 3

Reading: Psalm 92

A white haired, slightly stooped gentleman faithfully arrived at church every Sunday. Visually impaired, and with a tendency to be forgetful, he would stand and sing the hymns from memory. When there was a social evening he would often recite a favourite poem or two.

As a young minister in my first appointment this man was a great encouragement. As the passage in Psalm 92 stated, he was bearing fruit in his old age. Remember, fruit is not for the 'tree' to eat. Rather, what is produced is to nourish the life of others. How fortunate those who are recipients of this fruit. Is there a secret to growing it? The psalm says 'yes'! It is the result of a righteous life.

As Christians we realise no one is righteous. We all have failed the doing 'what is right in God's eyes' test. All, that is, except Jesus Christ! He is declared to have measured up to God's rigorous and unbending Law by His resurrection from the dead. (Romans 1:1-4). This means, in the words of 1 Corinthians 1:30: 'He is the source of your life in Christ Jesus, who became for us wisdom from God, and righteousness and sanctification and redemption.'

In Psalm 92 the righteous are portrayed as two types of trees. At a cursory reading the significance of these examples may not be clear. Both the palm and cedar trees are closely linked with the temple of God built by Solomon. In this meditation we will major on the palm tree and its personal implications.

1 Kings 6:29: 'He carved the walls of the house all around with carved engravings of cherubim, palm trees and open flowers, in the inner and outer rooms.' The temple experienced and expressed the presence of the Lord God of Hosts. His eyes were on it continually. The engravings of the palm trees must have delighted Him, not because of their artistry, but for their symbolism. Yahweh was reminded of His faithful people who would dwell in His presence.

In the Middle East the palm tree is a vital source of life. It endures harsh conditions, yet produces nutritious dates. Other trees are more decorative and fragile. The palm tree is always green and supplied with sap. Do we have here an inkling of God's planting and power supply for His servants?

He has many a 'palm tree' in hostile environments. Simply by being who they are, often without a word spoken, they proclaim that the Lord is upright. Who knows the number of people that these faithful nurture and nourish? Proverbs 11:30: 'The fruit of the righteous is a tree of life'. Without them, the ungodly would be bereft of the food which produces faith leading to salvation.

According to the Psalmist the palm and the cedar are precious to the Lord. So much so, they are planted within His house and courtyard. What an honour! Can you imagine Him walking in His house as though it was the Garden of Eden? He who sought out the company of the first couple still seeks out those whose hearts are set upon Him. The Lord enjoys His people. As Jesus Himself said, He wants them to be with Him in glory. Psalm 146:8c: 'The Lord loves the righteous'.

The engravings on the temple walls indicated the desire of the Lord. He isn't really interested in still art as much as the living expression to which the carvings pointed. As Proverbs 14:9 so aptly puts it: 'The upright enjoy God's favour'.

Ageless: 'Blessed are those who trust in the Lord. They shall be like a tree planted by the water, sending out its roots by the stream. It shall not fear when heat comes, and its leaves shall stray green; in the year of drought it is not anxious, and it does not cease to bear fruit.' Psalm 1.

God's Self Assessment Chart
Day 4

Reading: 1 Timothy 3:1-7

I've been helped by personality assessment sheets. I've been given insights from temperament charts. They also have been a curse and a hindrance. They lock you into a prefigured understanding. This is like a mental straight jacket when considering how you view yourself and how you view others.

A wonderful thing about the work of Christ is how He overrules these descriptions and restrictions. Regardless of our personality type and screwed up temperaments, our Lord calls us to aspire to a heavenly standard. As we mature there should be a desire to reach it. One of the sad things I have noticed in ministry is the lack of motivation to be the best type of person for the Lord. One young man was content to accept salvation, but retain his own sovereignty with its low level of behaviour. His life made sad reading.

The Bible spells out the quality of life Christ Jesus desires. The set reading is a summary. Run your personality and temperament across the Biblical assessment of a dynamic senior servant. It's a call to rise above mediocrity and escape the folly of excuses. Dynamic living begins with the desire to aspire. Wrapped up in this word is the motivation to reach out for it. This requires an act of will, not simply some emotional whim. Underlying this act of will is the sense of being grateful to the Lord. His mercy inspires a compulsion to live in ways which please Him. Here are some goals to aim for:

To be above reproach! This is a proactive response to the open and obedient lifestyle the Lord delights in. It's saying that we are not hiding behind masks or deceit. The Lord knows that, as we grow in the Christian life, we will make mistakes. He has provided for that. Our repentance before Him and restitution to others verifies how genuine we are in our commitment to Christ Jesus. The soul may bear scars from the healing of forgiveness; it shouldn't have ulcers of unrepentance. Sometimes the transformed life takes years of testing before people who know us accept what Jesus has done in us. The transparent quality of our life and deeds will ultimately be appreciated by friend and foe.

The words *'temperate, sensible, respectable, hospitable'* all have links to being above reproach. Each requires us to be put under the microscope of people's knowledge of us and our faith. They may not like Christians or the Gospel but they should have no charges to make against us. Some, out of spite, may manufacture stories to harm our reputation but our behaviour should reveal their vindictiveness. 1 Peter 3:16.

A married Christian man has an added challenge. *'He is to manage his own household well'.* In this intense relationship he is to express the love of Christ in meaningful ways (Ephesians 5:25-31). This will be fashioned within various cultural environments. To manage his family and be an inspiration to his children is no small task. By setting his heart on achieving this he will be investing treasure into his wife and children. Part of this will be their desire to aspire to a similar dynamic life.

Looking back to the days I went to Sunday school, it was the character of a couple of men who created a thirst within me. I had many rough years growing up, but I wanted to be like them. They didn't say the words of Philippians 4:9 to me, but they lived out the challenge. 'Keep on doing the things that you have learned and received and heard and seen in me, and the God of peace will be with you.' By the grace of God, that aspiration has not been quenched. The peace God promised is meant to be ours also.

The passage under consideration is, of course, giving instruction for selecting bishops for the local church. Not every man will reach it, but Scripture doesn't limit it to successful candidates. Essentially, what is written is an outline of God's mature and godly disciple. Every young person should have the desire to be such a man in his mature years. Naturally, the principles also apply to Christ's female disciples.

Every ageing believer, man or woman, should aim to repeat, in their own words, what Paul said in 2 Timothy 3:10 & 14: 'Now you have observed my teaching, my conduct, my aim in life, my faith, my patience, my love, my steadfastness ... (so) continue in what you have learned and firmly believed, knowing from whom you learned it.'

Ageless: 'Let no one despise your youth (or ageing), but set the believers an example in speech and conduct, in love, in faith, in purity.' 1 Timothy 4:12.

An Invitation Too Good to Miss
Day 5

Reading: 1 Kings 19:1-18

'Come to me, all you that are weary and are carrying heavy burdens and I will give you rest'. Matthew 11:28.

That's me, Lord! I'm weary on a number of fronts. I guess it is something to do with ageing. Whatever caused it, I've been overtaken by weariness. Some of the reasons are self inflicted and pleasant, such as minding my grandchildren. Others are not so pleasant. I'm weary from trying to do good to ungrateful people. When I try and share what you have done for me and them they couldn't care less. And Lord, I get so weary in praying. Why? Because so little seems to change in the lives of people and their circumstances!

I've checked out your Word, Lord Jesus, on this matter. What did I find? Galatians 6:9: 'Let us not grow weary in doing what is right, for we will reap at harvest time, if we do not give up.' Lord, I don't want to give up. Perhaps I need to take up your offer and come into your presence. What would I do there? Simply enjoy you and rest in your company.

Is this the way my ageing process can maintain its spiritual dynamics. May it be so! I know my physical energy is less than it once was. Guilty feelings sneak over me when I read Isaiah 40:29–31: 'He gives power to the faint, and strengthens the powerless. Those who wait for the Lord shall renew their strength, they shall mount up with wings like eagles, they shall run and not be weary, they shall walk and not faint.'

That's not me, Lord, at least not always! Can I ask what you are trying to get across to me and perhaps to others like me? Surely those verses contain a promise for something beyond the normal daily demands. I'm saying this because of what I read about You in John 4:6: 'Jacob's well was there (in Sychar in Samaria), and Jesus, tired out by his journey, was sitting by the well. It was about noon.'

Am I right in thinking this is where Isaiah 40 became your own personal experience? You were tired, but when that woman came You rose up to minister to her. I believe You were refreshed by more than adrenalin. Was it the Holy Spirit who gave You the energy to run, walk and rise on those 'eagle's wings' the prophet wrote about? Such a reality is evident within the words You spoke to your disciples: 'I have food to eat that you do not know about' (John 4:32).

We all get weary in the course of living and especially in ministry. Suddenly we are confronted with a surprising situation, whether good or evil. We are required to climb over our tiredness and grapple with the matter. The account in Luke 5 is illuminating. The fishermen had been out all night without the proverbial 'bite'. I'm sure they were tired, hungry and ready for a well deserved sleep. You appeared on the scene and gave a command wrapped up in a suggestion: 'Put out into the deep water and let down your nets for a catch.' More effort, more time, but also more reward. I'm sure they would have slept well later.

Lord, You have called us into a dynamic relationship with yourself. That means whether young, middle aged or older, we can express that dynamic life according to our years. I feel much more comfortable when I realise that my weariness is understandable to You. Help me to grasp the wonder of your grace which enables me to be refreshed to handle the issues that confront me.

Ageless: A promise to Israel for a future time can be applied to us today: 'I will satisfy the weary and all who faint I will replenish' Jeremiah 31:25.

The Beauty of Grey Hair
Day 6

Reading: Proverbs 16:31–33

An intriguing statement is recorded in Proverbs 20:29: 'The glory of youths is their strength, but the beauty of the aged is their grey hair.'

Let your mind dwell on that for a moment or two. Ask yourself the question — 'What's beautiful about grey hair?' I'd never really thought about it before. That's the stimulating power of proverb and parable. A germ of an idea burrows into the brain and, over time, concepts emerge to motivate or instruct.

Undoubtedly, the author is making a contrast. Those of us in our senior years can appreciate the strength and vitality of youth. Many of us may be scratching grey but thinning hair, or even a bald head, and wondering about it. What is beautiful about old age? I'm equating the author of Proverbs use of grey hair as a metaphor for being old.

As I passed through adolescence to adulthood I was captivated by the faces of older people. Their wrinkles told stories. Their eyes could sparkle or be in faraway places. Frail bodies did not speak of fragility, but of bearing life's pressure. Old they were, but in mind, spirit or outlook they were not stagnant. To sit in their presence, even in the company of the grumpy ones, was fascinating. I wouldn't have called it beautiful, but that's what it was.

In the midst of those ageing people I've met over the years it became apparent that in some lives there was a different bearing. All had their heartbreaks, sorrows and joys and wore the signs in their hearts and on their faces. Yet there were those men and women whose faces shone!

It is said about couples who have spent a lifetime together 'they resemble each other'. In some cases it might have an outward manifestation, but I think it is best sensed, rather than seen. The two individuals may be unaware that others sense this in them. There is a spiritual truth wrapped up in that principle. The more time you spend in the presence of another the more it becomes apparent.

Consider Moses. He went into the presence of Yahweh on Mount Sinai for forty days. Coming back into the company of the nation, Moses was unaware of a radiance glowing from his face (Exodus 34:29-35). The people saw it. They knew its source. The first martyr of the Church, Stephen, was charged with blasphemy and called upon to defend himself. After hearing the words of false witnesses he is described in Acts 6:15: 'All who sat in council looked intently at him, and they saw that his face was like the face of an angel.'

Stephen didn't reach old age. His story, however, reveals the beauty of combining a journey by faith in Christ Jesus and the inner radiance which seeps out. The word used for 'beauty' in Proverbs 20:29 carries a strong relationship to God. It is translated by such words as excellence, glory, honour, majesty. Psalm 104:1: 'Bless the Lord, O my soul. O Lord my God, You are very great. You are clothed with honour and majesty.' Psalm 29:4: 'The voice of the Lord is powerful; the voice of the Lord is full of majesty.' To my mind there is a link between the glory of the Lord and the beauty of grey hairs. The connection takes place as the Lord and the believer share time together in His word. This relationship grows stronger across the years, even as the hair turns grey or becomes less.

Ageless: 'What are human beings that you are mindful of them, mortals that you care for them? Yet you have made them a little lower than God, and crowned them with glory and honour. You have given them dominion over the works of your hands ...' Psalm 8:4-6.

Caleb
Day 7

Reading: Joshua 14:6-15

He was eighty-five and spoiling for a fight. It was over forty-five years in the making. The original contest was denied by the nation's unbelief (Numbers 13-14). Now he and Joshua were the only two of that generation left. Together, with the second generation, they had claimed the promise of God to Abraham. This was after forty years of wandering and five years of conquest.

Now Caleb wanted to claim the personal possession promised him. Joshua 14:9: 'Moses swore on that day, saying, "Surely the land on which your foot has trodden shall be an inheritance for you and your children forever, because you have wholeheartedly followed the Lord my God".'

Guess who was waiting to do battle with him? The descendents of the same race that made the ten spies afraid! Their report influenced the nation so much that it said 'no' to going in. So God accepted their decision, reluctantly, I imagine. The children twenty years and under would possess it instead. Now Caleb could follow through on his statement of faith forty-five years earlier. Numbers 13:30: 'Let us go up at once and occupy it, for we are well able to overcome it.' Now, instead of relying upon the whole nation, Caleb took his tribe of Judah to accomplish the conquest of Hebron.

To me, Caleb expressed the dynamic combination of faith and ageing. Whether you take his words 'I am still as strong today as I was on the day that Moses sent me (to spy out the land) …' as fact or hyperbole, he was itching to claim the promise. In fact, what he had witnessed of God's faithfulness over the past four and a half decades must have strengthened his resolve.

What are some of those 'God encounters' which strengthened Caleb's spirit as weary day succeeded weary day? The manna from heaven; water from the rock, twice; the bronze serpent and the healing of those bitten; the budding of Aaron's rod to show the Lord God's appointed high priest from among others vying for the position. Those and many others would have undergirded his trust in the Lord to fulfil His promise. We should take this to heart as we confront delays in seeing God fulfil His promises. Have you felt that the unbelief, stubbornness and folly of others delayed some promise of God to you personally? Don't surrender to resentment. Hang in there with the confidence that the Lord keeps His word. This is the only way you will be able to resist being bitter, negative, even vindictive towards those who frustrated your hopes.

We have no idea how long Caleb lived after entering the land that was given to him. Whether long or short, he would have been able to stand on the highest mountain and yell, 'I told you so! God is faithful and I'm enjoying His promise to the full.' What a testimony it would have been to his family and the upcoming generation.

He has left for us a wonderful legacy to inspire us in our ageing. Caleb used a descriptive statement when challenging his countrymen to trust the Lord and go conquer the land. Numbers 14:8: 'If the Lord is pleased with us, he will bring us into this land and give it to us ...' the majority displeased the Lord and missed out. The verdict of God on Caleb is recorded by his possession of the promise. I believe Caleb's words still hold true for you and me today.

Ageless: 'There is still a vision for the appointed time, it speaks of the end, and does not lie. If it seems to tarry, wait for it; it will surely come, it will not delay'. Habakkuk 2:3.

The Strength of Years
Day 8

Reading: 1 Kings 6:11–22

The king of the mountain is the claim for the cedar tree. This Biblical aristocrat inhabits the snow kissed mountains of Lebanon and elsewhere. In Psalm 92 it is mentioned with the palm tree decorating Solomon's temple. The word for cedar comes from the Arabic meaning strength. Associated with the palm tree we may see the symbolism of fruitfulness and strength.

As we reflect upon this symbolism and associate it with old age and spirituality it may seem a strange combination. Physical strength is not something usually associated with senior years. Therefore, combining the two must mean so much more than sheer muscle power. From the Biblical understanding, true strength is measured by our faithfulness to truth. It means endurance when we're under pressure to recant and wisdom in obeying God's word amidst confused situations.

1 Kings 6 records the building of the temple. Cedar is prominent in both the seen and unseen construction. It was used for the beams and planks from the floor to the rafters. Engraved within the wood were gourds and open flowers, whilst the altar was overlaid with it.

How awesome is the symbolism and its place within the household of God (1 Timothy 3:15). The godly aged, represented by the cedar, provide strength accumulated from years of knowing Christ Jesus. There is also a fragrance which permeates their lifestyle, ministry and worship. The source is none other than Christ Himself (2 Corinthians 2:14-16). A unique feature of the cedars of Lebanon was in its resin. This meant it had a wide variety of uses, from ship building to musical instruments, as well as household furniture. How was this possible? It was incorruptible!

In 2 Peter 1:2-4 the apostle elaborates on the source of our inner incorruptibleness. 'May grace and peace be yours in abundance in the knowledge of God and of Jesus our Lord. His divine power has given us everything needed for life and godliness, through the knowledge of him who called us by his own glory and goodness. Thus he has given us, through these things, his precious and very great promises, so that through them you may escape from the corruption that is in the world because of lust, and may become participants of the divine nature.' Our strength as ageing believers comes from our intimate knowledge and faith relationship with our Lord. We know, don't we, where this knowledge is found!

1 Kings 6:18 informs us that there were engravings of gourds and open flowers in the cedar. As the Lord doesn't do anything without a reason what can we make of these? Gourds are not edible. They are used for practical purposes, such as bowls, cups, bottles and other utensils. I'm reminded of what Paul said in 2 Timothy 2:20 'In a large house there are utensils not only of gold and silver but also of wood and clay, some for special use, some for ordinary ... All who cleanse themselves ... will become special utensils, dedicated and useful to the owner of the house, ready for every good work.' God's requirement for service doesn't depend on outstanding ability or age, but on being set apart by Him to fulfil His purposes.

What can we make of the 'open flowers'? All references to flowers speak of a beauty which isn't permanent. 'As for mortals, their days are like grass; they flourish like a flower of the field; for the wind passes over it, and it is gone.' (Psalm 103:15-16). Could the engravings be a reminder about our brevity of life and that only in Christ Jesus do we have eternal life? All this points to the truth that, though our bodies are wearing away, there is within us an undying strength. What a wonderful hope awaits when that strength is clothed with a new body. The miracle of grace and the power of Calvary is how the Lord transforms human 'weeds' and 'bramble' into His plantings. Our wonderful Saviour sees us as 'palms or cedars' fit for adorning His house.

Ageless: 'Our citizenship is in heaven. We eagerly await a Saviour from there, the Lord Jesus Christ, who, by the power that enables Him to bring everything under His control, will transform our lowly bodies so that they will be like His glorious body.' Philippians 3:20-21.

Don't Chase the Wind
Day 9

Reading: Ecclesiastes 3:1–14

The teacher, as the author of Ecclesiastes calls himself, writes a review of his life. From all indications he has lived long, lived well and lived fruitlessly. To read his story is depressing and challenging. Today, in our materialistic and pleasure seeking world, he would probably be considered a celebrity.

Ecclesiastes is not a Biblical book that is read by many people. It should be, especially by young adults. Read through the teacher's experiences of fame, fortune and frustration. Cry at a wasted life in the light of life's end. Of course there are positive statements such as love your wife, enjoy your labour, but over all it's a lamentation.

One of the most worthwhile things he did was to spell out his experiences. Writing for the young he sounds a warning. Ecclesiastes 11:9: 'Follow the inclination of your heart and the desire of your eyes, but know that for all these things God will bring you into judgment.' Was the teacher inferring a sow and reap sequence? He understood the grave as life's full-stop, therefore judgement must take place somehow, sometime. Jesus is the one who takes us beyond the grave and reveals the individual's accountability. This takes place before the heavenly throne of God.

The word 'vanity' is used in this book thirty-four times. What a sad epithet this makes on a person's resume of his or her life. The word 'vanity' speaks of meaninglessness. To live without reference to the Lord God of Hosts is also likened to 'a chasing after the wind'. A footnote to this phrase indicates it could also be written as 'feeding on wind'. Either way, such a lifestyle is unsatisfying in time or eternity. Unfortunately, it is the main, perhaps the only diet of the soul many feast upon. Jesus said in John 10:10: 'I came that they might have life, and have it abundantly.' However, Christ Jesus offers this life in what may be described as brown paper wrapping. It is sealed with the cross. Inside the package called abundant life is found incomparable treasures of grace and glory. It seems to me Jesus offered His spiritual and eternal wealth to those who fall in love with Him for who He is. Faithful obedience opens the wrapping.

In contrast the world presents its version of life in glossy wrapping with glittering sequins to capture the eye and steal the heart. What is inside is a mirage that leads to 'vanity, vanity, all is vanity.' Jesus puts it another way in Matthew 16:24: 'What will it profit them if they gain the whole world but forfeit their life? Or what will they give in return for their life?'

Regret is the price for the follies and choices of youth. We need not allow our vanity and chasing after 'wind' to haunt our ageing. The offer of Jesus to give abundant life has no age limit. There are many whose senior years have been transformed by placing their remaining years into Christ's care. Forgiveness for the past and hope in the future gives a joy and thankfulness in the present. Vanity is erased and is replaced by purpose with passion. They know they are precious to the Lord as the cross and resurrection declared.

The Teacher closes his writing with a motivational appeal to fear God and obey his commands. So true! What he seems to be saying is 'Don't do what I've done, do what I'm saying from what I've learnt.' How much more inspirational would it have been for him to say: 'You see my footsteps and where they're leading. Come follow me. I have found Him who is the author and completer of life! His name is Jesus.'

Regardless of how long we have had Jesus Christ as our Lord and Saviour there should be a song in our hearts. No longer is there the lament of the teacher so sadly written in Ecclesiastes. Now the Hallelujah chorus is rehearsed in our daily lives for the choir in the sky.

Ageless: 'Do not love the world or the things in the world. The love of the Father is not in those who love the world ... the world and its desire are passing away, but those who do the will of God live forever.' 1 John 2:15-17.

Taming the Lions
Day 10

Reading: Psalm 57

My first memory of Daniel in the lions' den story was a picture of this young man calmly sitting with them in their dungeon. This, I learnt later, was a false representation. When Daniel was introduced to the lions he was a much older man.

There appears from Daniel's experiences a pattern which confronts all of us in life. This is true whether we are Christians or not. As we grow older life has a way of placing heavier burdens on us. If they had come when we were younger in age or faith we may well have buckled. Proving that God is with us in the little trials and tribulations lays a foundation which will not crack when harsher times come. This is one of the lessons from Daniel's life. After being taken as a captive to Babylon with his three friends he faced a tough decision. Would they eat the food supplied by the king? Was it, could it be ceremonially clean, according to the strict Jewish food laws?

On the surface it doesn't seem to be much to worry about. However, it involved their dedication to Yahweh. Daniel's conscience and faith forced him to make a stand. In similar ways each of us are challenged in the early days of our commitment to Christ with apparent innocuous choices. On the surface there doesn't appear to be any harm but ... Would our choice be detrimental in some unforseen way to our faith, conscience and witness? Taking a stand then and proving God faithful was, in fact, the basis for handling the lions in old age. He would have been in his early teens when he had to choose his diet and prove God faithful.

In Daniel 6 there are two types of lions. There are the actual four legged beasts and the men who symbolise them. Daniel probably found the four legged animals much more congenial than the other. Daniel's statement to King Darius would apply however in both instances. 'My God sent his angel and shut the lions' mouths so they would not hurt me, because I was found blameless before him.'

It is highly unlikely any of us will be on the king of the jungle's menu. We will, unfortunately, have to deal with their symbolic relatives. Such people may want to devour far more than our faith. It could stem from jealousy, racial prejudices, real or imagined offences and religious hostility, among other matters. Whatever the reason you may feel like David in Psalm 57:4: 'I lie down among lions that greedily devour human prey; their teeth are spears and arrows, their tongues sharp swords.' The only guarantee that we will prevail will be traced back to how well we have found the Lord faithful in earlier years.

Strewn over life's landscape are the moral and spiritual 'skeletons' of too many disciples. Was this due to their inability to tame the lions in their scene? Was their failure because they chose the rich fare promised by a godless society? Compromise at the beginning will make you a potential victim for the lions in coming years. In Psalm 10:9 the psalmist likens the wicked to lions intent upon devouring the poor. May I be allowed to define the poor in this devotional as those without a treasure chest of knowing Christ's grace and faithfulness?

Lions prey on the weak and vulnerable, not the strong and healthy. In my Sunday school days I learnt a song, *Dare to be a Daniel*. It is only in much later years I realise why we must dare to be a Daniel. To remain committed, consecrated and convinced about Christ Jesus means trusting the Lord. How? By honouring Him through faith choices early in your Christian life! Such choices will be in harmony with His character and word. They are not easy. They do, however, prepare you for when the lions roam and roar.

Ageless: The Lord stood by me and gave me strength, so that through me the message might be fully proclaimed and all the Gentiles might hear it. So I was rescued from the lion's mouth. The Lord will rescue me from every attack and save me for his heavenly kingdom. To him be glory forever and ever. Amen. 2 Timothy 4:17-18.

Making Sure everything is in Order
Day 11

Reading: 1 Corinthians 3:10-15

When our working years have run their course new opportunities emerge for leisure, adventure and hobbies. There is one other aspect so often overlooked in the rush to fill up the new realm. Ageing offers us the time for reflection and to get 'dressed' properly to meet our Lord and Saviour.

'Whether we are at home or away, we make it our aim to please him. For all of us must appear before the judgement seat of Christ, so that each may receive recompense for what has been done in the body, whether good or evil.' (2 Corinthians 5:9-10). This isn't for salvation approval. That was guaranteed when we accepted Christ as Lord and Saviour. It means we are to give an account of our faithfulness to Him across our Christian life.

Many conflicting pressures would have been upon us during the years preceding our retirements. Some vows may not have been properly fulfilled, opportunities missed, stewardship squandered. Perhaps now we can make amends. I would like us to consider three areas to brush up on as the time of appearing before our Lord draws near.

The first area is put to us from 2 Peter 3:18: 'Grow in the grace and knowledge of our Lord and Saviour Jesus Christ'. Would you say your knowledge of the Lord is deeper and richer now than ten years ago? Is it stagnant or crowded out by temporal concerns? How can we grow in the unmerited kindness of God? By knowing and doing what His Word says. Within the Scriptures we can find God's will for us *all our lives*. As we obey what He says the Holy Spirit will also impress upon our heart and mind something specific for us to do or be. What a privilege we have in our ageing when we become men or women of dynamic growth.

The second area comes from John 15:8: 'My Father is glorified by this, that you bear much fruit and become my disciples.' Any orchardist knows that between the budding, the bloom and the bearing of fruit are many obstacles and enemies. The same applies to our spiritual fruitfulness in the Lord. The fruit of the Spirit which we bear in our lives may be affected by the frost of our self-obsession. The fruit of righteousness may have been spoilt by 'bugs' of indifference. Our present period of life allows us to pay more careful attention to bearing 'fruit' worthy for the Father's pleasure. Always keep in mind the fruit the Lord wants to produce in our lives is for others. It isn't for the 'tree'!

The third area to come to our attention is 1 Corinthians 4:2: 'Moreover, it is required of stewards that they be found trustworthy.' The Lord God has invested a tremendous amount of energy into our lives. Each of us has received natural, as well as spiritual, gifts. They have been entrusted into our care. He is looking forward to receiving spiritual dividends in and through our faithful use. What do these dividends look like? A personal lifestyle which pleases Him, our family honouring the Lord, the fellowship of His people encouraged by our involvement in worship and stewardship.1 Peter 4:10: 'Like good stewards of the manifold grace of God, serve one another with whatever gift each of you has received.'

Whatever our limitations with health, family and locations, we have the chance to do a bit of 'scrubbing up' and polishing of our appearance. It is exciting to know that the Lord wants to join you in your preparation. He supplies the resources of His grace so that you will not to be ashamed in His company. Jude 24: 'Now to him who is able to keep you from falling, *and to make you stand without blemish in the presence of his glory with rejoicing ...*' (emphasis added).

Ageless: I sought the Lord, and he answered me, and delivered me from all my fears. Look to him, and be radiant; so your faces shall never be ashamed.' (Psalm 34:4-5).

Give Thanks for the Rooster
Day 12

Reading: Luke 22:31-34, 54-62

Did the apostle Peter place a drawing of a rooster on his wall? Remember it was the cock crowing which broke his heart. He would always remember the words of Jesus, 'I tell you, Peter, the cock will not crow this day, until you have denied three times that you know me.'

Why would Peter have fond memories of such an embarrassing failure of courage? Because it was the making of the man! He who would quake at a maiden's question would introduce the Gospel on Pentecost Sunday. He would face prison and threats unbowed in his commitment to Christ Jesus. From self confidence and the bravery of arrogance, this Galilean would emerge stronger. From the time of the rooster Peter became a wiser, humbler and faithful servant of Jesus Christ.

Do you look back on similar soul crushing experiences and thank God for them? At the time it seemed to be the end of the world. Would it cancel our relationship with the Lord and Saviour Jesus? Slowly you realise what Peter found after Christ's resurrection. Jesus makes a special point of coming to you. On reflection did you discover a deeper devotion because of His grace to you through your darkest moment? I must confess that is how it worked out in my life.

What is the purpose for allowing us to go through such travail and disillusionment of faith and commitment? Psalm 34:18: 'The Lord is near to the broken–hearted, and saves the crushed in spirit.' David later understood his words in a deeper way as he emerged from a moral failure. Psalm 51:17: 'The sacrifice acceptable to God is a broken spirit; a broken and contrite heart, O God, you will not despise.'

Writing his second letter to the scattered disciples, Peter tells them his date with death is drawing near. He wants to make sure they have a legacy from him in matters of faith. 2Peter 1:15: 'I will make every effort so that after my departure you may be able at any time to recall these things.' What were those things so important to his heart he had to share them? They centred in the person of Jesus Christ and the authority of the scriptures. He was also at pains to warn them of corrupt teachers masquerading as disciples. Then Peter sums up the wonder of the Christian hope: Jesus is returning one day, be ready!

The dynamism surrounding our ageing should vibrate with a similar confidence. Because of it we need to consider leaving a legacy of faith, hope and love for family and friends to draw upon. There are various ways of doing this. Write out your testimony concerning your salvation. Recall and record some of your experiences of Christ Jesus' grace and providence. The truth of your life will be proof of your words.

There is something special about picking up an account of your parent, grandparent or other relation and reading their story. From the perspective of the Christian faith there is the added sense of awe after reading their faith journey. If you are the first in your known family line to be a disciple of Christ, what a marvellous privilege you have. You are the Lord's life changing, destiny altering agent of His Holy Spirit into following generations.

As I read Peter's first letter I think I hear the rooster's echo. Perhaps when others read or hear your story the reality of your brokenness will flavour it without you ever mentioning it. Do you hear the 'cock' when Peter wrote, 'Always be ready to make your defence to anyone who demands from you an accounting for the hope that is in you.' (1 Peter 3:15). Maybe its sound is in chapter 5:6-7: 'Humble yourselves therefore under the mighty hand of God, so that he may exalt you in due time. Cast all your anxiety on him, because he cares for you. Discipline yourselves, keep alert.'

Ageless: Rejoice in the ministry of Jesus prophesied in Isaiah 61:1: 'The spirit of the Lord God is upon me, because the Lord has anointed me; He has sent me to bring good news to the oppressed, to *bind up the broken–hearted* (emphasis added), to proclaim liberty to the captives, and release to the prisoners.'

God Rules from the Shadows
Day 13

Reading: James 1:1–12

Esther is one of the most interesting books in the Old Testament. One of the reasons is the fact that the name of God is nowhere explicitly mentioned. As you read the account of the principle players in the historical drama you sense God. He is there. He is in the shadows. He is overruling.

Is the Lord God trying to impress something important on our minds through this book? Without a doubt! What is it, especially in relation to us in our senior years? We each have our histories and the fallout from choices and bad decisions made by ourselves or others. Unprincipled people in power and vindictive hatred arising from corrupt egos fall heavily on God's people. And in all fairness let it be said, on others without faith also! The cry goes up 'Where is God in all of this? It's unfair!'

Mordecai could have uttered that cry. If he did it isn't recorded. Somehow I don't think he was of such a frame of mind. Taken captive from Israel by Nebuchanezzar's forces he was now living in Shushan. One interpretation of his name says it means 'little man'. This is significant. Why? 1 Corinthians 1:28-29: 'God chose what is low and despised in the world, things that are not, to reduce to nothing things that are, so that no one might boast in the presence of God.'

As you read the book it is clear this man, old and either retired or unemployed, turns up at some critical moments. He adopted Esther, his cousin, who was an orphan. Through a chain of events she is chosen to be Ahasuerus's queen without the king knowing she was Jewish. When Mordecai learnt of the plot by a government official to exterminate the Jewish people, Mordecai put his cousin in the hot seat. She must reveal her race. She must pave the way to save her people.

The words of this 'little man' were true then and remain true always. Esther 4:14: 'If you keep silence at such a time as this, relief and deliverance will rise for the Jews from another quarter, but you and your father's family will perish. Who knows? Perhaps you have come to royal dignity for just such a time as this.' The festival of Purim, celebrated every year by the nation of Israel, speaks of Esther's faithfulness. It validates Mordecai's confidence.

Many are the lessons in that historical account for us. The Christian Faith is being assailed and vilified by the world powers. You personally may be going through tough, even rotten times. We look for God, but there isn't any vision. Maybe we should be asking, 'Has God put me here for just such a time as this?' Mordecai's Jewish background gave him the backbone to stand and not to collapse. That's the Lord's intention also for us through our Christian faith.

Most of us are in the same league as Mordecai. We are 'little men', 'little women'. That is comforting. It allows the Lord to express Himself from the shadows in and through us for the salvation of someone, or the upholding of God's unchanging and absolute Truth. At the same time, we are declaring our confidence in the God who keeps His Word. This assurance underpins Romans 8:28: 'We know that all things work together for good for those who love God, who are called according to his purpose.' Such confidence eases the pain of the tough, unexplainable times. It is saying God hasn't forgotten. The shadows of your situation may hide Him, but He is acting on your behalf.

Ageless: 'Even though I walk through the darkest valley I fear no evil; for you are with me; your rod and your staff – they comfort me.' Psalm 23:4.

Key Words for the Ageing — #1: Inheritance
Day 14

Reading: 1 Peter 1:1-9

An inheritance is what we leave to another or others upon confirmation of our death. To have something to bequeath indicates that, over your lifetime, you have accumulated worthwhile possessions. As I write this I have to ask myself what have I accumulated that is worth bestowing upon my children or others? Will it be cherished or squandered? Has it a use by date or will it be treasured for a lifetime? Does it have the smell of dust or of eternity?

One of the wonderful things the Christian faith speaks about is an eternal inheritance. That means something waits beyond the grave. I cannot earn it, for it is an inheritance. The offer is strictly for 'family members in the Kingdom of God'. How depressing! The unrighteous will never possess that Kingdom. In my moments of honest reflection I know that used to include me. What changed all that? Colossians 1:12-14: 'Giving thanks to the Father, who has enabled you to share in the inheritance of the saints in the light. He has rescued us from the power of darkness and transferred us into the kingdom of his beloved Son, in whom we have redemption, the forgiveness of sins.'

Whose accumulated possessions and everlasting kingdom have we inherited? Christ Jesus'! We know this, yet rarely do we appreciate the magnitude of His grace towards us. For us to receive this gift, the death of the owner, the King of the kingdom, was required! His death meant He had to participate in our world. It needed to be confirmed, recorded and heralded. This is the Gospel of Jesus Christ. This is the record of the Bible. This is the testimony of the Church. This is affirmed by history.

Many are the reasons why Jesus had to come and to die. Some of them are presented in my previous books, *Captured by Calvary* and *Bethlehem's Warrior Baby*. For the purpose of this devotion we consider Galatians 1:3-4: Grace and peace from God our Father and the Lord Jesus Christ, who gave himself for our sins to set us free from the present evil age, according to the will of our God and Father.' What a privilege we have experienced by responding to the message of the cross.

The inheritance you and I leave has little bearing on who we are or were. From out of our estate creditors will need to be repaid and other expenses covered. Whatever the beneficiaries may receive is not dependent upon us coming back to life. This is, without doubt, the requirement for us to possess our inheritance from God. Everything rides on Christ rising from the power of the tomb and the clutches of death. From the many passages verifying this fact of history I've chosen 1 Peter 1:3-4: 'Blessed be the God and Father of our Lord Jesus Christ! By his mercy he has given us a new birth into a living hope through the resurrection of Jesus Christ from the dead.'

Who He is? What He has done? What He has promised? What we have become, and therefore our promised inheritance, is linked and inseparable from the fact that Christ Jesus rose from the dead. Paul summarises it in 1 Corinthians 15:17: 'If Christ has not been raised your faith is futile and you are still in your sins.' Simply put, we remain unrighteous, unforgiven and unable to receive any eternal inheritance. The Easter declaration still sounds: 'Why do you look for the living among the dead? He is not here, but has risen.' Jesus has redeemed us from our debt to God's law, paid the wages of our sin, removed our unrighteousness, clothed us with His righteousness and adopted us into His family and kingdom.

What waits now is the Lord's call to come in and enjoy what He has made possible. Until then we are to get to know Him more and more through His word, worship and service.

Ageless: 'We want each of you to … realise the full assurance of hope to the very end, so that you may not become sluggish, but imitators of those who through faith and patience inherit the promises.' Hebrews 6:11-12.

Courageous Ageing
Day 15

Reading: Joshua 1:1-9

They came suddenly. They struck swiftly at the rear of the marching people. It was a deadly assault. To meet this crisis, Moses chose Joshua. Up until that moment this man isn't mentioned in Scripture. He must have made his presence felt somehow or other. It was probably, as Scripture insists, by being faithful in the little things. That meant he could be trusted with something greater.

How old was this man? Probably in his forties. Now he is called upon to take up the sword. At this stage of his life the Lord marks him out for leadership. In many ways such a pattern is being repeated in the lives of many dedicated believers today. It is thrilling to read of professional men and women leaving their well paid positions to serve the Lord in specific areas.

When we open the book of Joshua we know both Caleb and he are thirty-eight years older. Moses has died and the national leadership is resting on Joshua's shoulders. In his eighties he leads the second generation of Israelites into the Promised Land. What is in store? Conflict! How great his stamina must have been. Surely he would have felt a little apprehensive. The Lord understood this and so three times in chapter one He encouraged His servant: 'Be strong and courageous; for you shall put this people in possession of the land I swore to their ancestors to give them.'(Joshua 1:6). As you read Israel's history and Joshua's part you realise he was a brave man. Now the Lord required a different type of bravery. Joshua was to be more than a warrior. He had to be the person responsible for securing the promise. Because He had trusted the Lord in the past, Joshua understood the Lord's trustworthiness.

Joshua 1:7: 'Only be strong and very courageous, being careful to act in accordance with all the law that my servant Moses commanded you.' Did you catch the specific emphasis? Why was he to be very courageous? Because Joshua was to act according to the Law of God expressed through

Moses. Joshua would have to do this in a nation renowned for its mumbling, grumbling and defeatist attitude.

Joshua 1:9: 'I hereby command you: Be strong and courageous, do not be frightened or dismayed, for the Lord your God is with you wherever you go.' Can you sense the build up? This verse is commissioning Joshua to invade the land. They faced stiff opposition, and in many ways were an untried army. As the leader he must have felt a little uneasy knowing that fortified cities and well equipped armies were ahead of him.

Are you able to discern a thread woven into those verses? Reflect on them. It begins with counting upon God to fulfil His Word. This was something Joshua had experienced personally for over forty years. Then this servant of the Lord is to express bravely his conviction in the truth of God's Law. He must live it out before a godless world that was opposed to him, and a fickle people accompanying him. The real source of Joshua's strength and courage would come from trusting in the Lord's companionship each and every day.

Here is unshakeable assurance for each of us as we seek to possess the promises of Christ. The same principles apply. We are called upon to exert our will to engage life's issues. We are to exercise our devotion through obedience to God's word. We are to be energised by the fact of the Holy Spirit's unfailing companionship.

It doesn't get easier to be a man or woman of faith as we age. There are many giants to face. They will shrink and scatter before us as we mature in those three areas of a godly relationship. Joshua died aged one hundred and ten. His legacy is bound up in those words 'Be strong and very courageous'!

Ageless: Be strong, and let your heart take courage, all you who wait for the Lord. Psalm 31:24.

The Testimony of the Walking Stick
Day 16

Reading: Genesis 28:10-22. 32:22-32

Cunning, courteous and clever defines Jacob to me. In the early years of his life an onlooker would have said that he had no spiritual merit. Being sent away from home for his health and safety, Jacob camped at Luz.

He encountered God in a dream. In it he heard the Lord promise a similar message of blessing as given to Abraham. When he awoke, Jacob called the place Bethel – the house of God. As the story unfolds you realise that nothing had changed. Jacob is still cunning, courteous and clever. An encounter with God and the reception of a promise was pushed to the background. That's what makes this man so real to me. This is what so many of us tend to do. We forget our emotional vow of the moment. God doesn't!

This conman of the Bible goes to his uncle's place and dwells there for twenty years. After that time, with two wives and eleven children, he sets off for home. But Esau is between him and home. The brother who was tricked out of the father's blessing was on his way to meet Jacob. Fear abounded. In turn, this created a previous non-existent prayer life. A 'God protect me and mine' type of petition.

In Genesis 32 is the account which marked the transformation of the self reliant, shrewd and double dealing character. If anyone was to write our faith journey I'm sure there would be a similar chapter included. Bit by bit, Jacob finds himself alone beside the brook Jabbok. The name is revealing. It means 'emptying', 'pouring out'.

He was alone and no longer young. He faced a threatening situation and was afraid. Within him, however, was born or aroused a spiritual newness. We read that a man came to him. He wrestled with the man all night. Jacob would not let the man go, which shows us something about his nature. Jacob knew there was something unique about his opponent and he demanded a blessing. It was given when the other person touched the hollow of Jacob's thigh. He also said Jacob had a new name, Israel: 'Prince with God'. This man with a new name called the place 'Peniel': the face of God.

Ever afterwards Jacob walked with a limp. A walking stick became his testimony to the life changing, destiny altering encounter with the Angel of the Lord. The dream's promise at Bethel could only happen after the wrestling match. Jacob returned to the place of his dream, but he was now changed. The walking stick and limp bore testimony to that.

Many of us in our youth knew a place similar to 'Bethel'. Unfortunately, we walked on from there with only a memory, not a transformation. God waited. He knew when and where we would be alone by the brook Jabbok. Then He would come and grapple with us to transform and rename us. In Matthew 5:29-30 is the Lord's equivalent of Jacob's touched thigh for us. The maimed life is our testimony to being made whole in the Lord's sight. When God touched us it is seen in our priorities, morality, words and relationships. The untouched may consider us losers. We know we are winners. The kingdom of God is open to those He has touched and whose walk is accompanied by a 'walking stick'.

The life of Jacob takes on new and thrilling, though sometimes sad, dimensions from Peniel. He is honoured in Scripture and is part of the wonderful statement 'The God of Abraham, Isaac and Jacob'. After our Peniel wrestle, the title we are privileged to be called by Jesus is 'His brothers and sisters'. (Hebrews 2:11)

Ageless: 'Whatever gains I had, these I have come to regard as loss because of Christ. More than that, I regard everything as loss because of the surpassing value of knowing Christ Jesus my Lord.' Philippians 3:7-8.

Personal Eucharist
Day 17

Reading: 1 Thessalonians 5:18

This must be one of the most difficult verses to put into practise in all of Scripture. If we skip it when we are converted, we miss out on its dynamism in the ageing process. Let's dissect the verse and investigate, briefly, the treasure it holds.

Give thanks in all circumstances.

Can Paul be serious? Give thanks when your home has been destroyed by a rampaging mob who hate Christians? Give thanks as grief's tears pour down your cheeks? Give thanks after hearing a bad diagnosis from the doctor? What is Paul saying to us?

First up, he did not say give thanks for all circumstances. His challenge is about the way a person responds *in* any type of situation. Expressing thanks is a response of faith. You are saying God is in it with you. You don't have to like it, understand it or try and be super-spiritual about it. It is your heart bowing before the Lord and proclaiming He is in control. He will work it out for good. Whatever happens you are saying, 'I'm trusting Him'.

The word for thanks is 'eucharist'. We associate this word with the Lord's Supper without drinking in its significance for Jesus. When He gave thanks He knew what was to come. Imagine if you can the devotion and trust required by Jesus in the Upper Room. He went through it all for each of us. Now in our circumstances He calls us to trust Him.

For this is the will of God in Christ for you.

God's will is not referring to the circumstances. It speaks about our giving thanks. There must be a purpose wrapped up in God's will for us. It offers a shield to our heart from encroaching bitterness or self-pity. Life is unkind and cruel regardless of a person's faith or lack of it. As Christians, the way we deal with our circumstances has implications for our trust in the goodness of our Lord. Here is the essential difference between a believer and a non-believer enduring similar circumstances. Life is tough and unfair but our Lord God is good.

Colossians 3:15: 'Let the peace of Christ rule in your hearts, to which indeed you were called in the one body, and be thankful'. To be thankful to Christ Jesus for your circumstances requires His indwelling peace. Such a quality of the spirit demands an understanding of who Jesus is and what He has done. You have come to know Him in the good and not so good times. Now, when the really rugged times hit, you might buckle a little, but you do not collapse. When peace rules, the lips can express gratitude!

Within the sacrificial system of Israel one expressed thanksgiving and wellbeing (Leviticus 7:11-13. 22:29). It was costly to express gratitude to God. The price of the animal, the time involved, plus the unleavened cakes and wafers spread with oil. When we think of us giving thanks in our circumstances can we turn it into an offering to the Lord? How? Each sacrifice in the tabernacle ritual speaks of Christ. Therefore, when we lift up our heart in thankfulness, it must be linked to the cross of Christ. If He could make His cross a 'eucharistic' testimony, then by His risen power Jesus will enable us to do the same. Philippians 4:6-7: 'Do not worry about anything, but in everything by prayer and supplication with thanksgiving let your requests be made know to God. And the peace of God, which surpasses all understanding, will guard your hearts and your minds in Christ Jesus.'

Ageless: 'I will praise the name of God with a song; I will magnify him with thanksgiving.' Psalm 69:30.

Key Words for the Ageing — #2: Years restored
Day 18

Reading: Joel 2:25-27

In the Bible locusts became a sign to Israel they had violated God's law. Deuteronomy 28:15,38: 'If you will not obey the Lord your God by diligently observing all his commandments ... then these curses shall come upon you and overtake you ... You shall carry much seed into the field but shall gather little in, for the locusts shall consume it.'

This really happened. The prophet Joel recounted their devastation upon the land of his day. He also used them as a symbol of an attacking, marauding army. It isn't the Lord's intention to leave His people, nation and especially Jerusalem, in such a wasted condition. Joel 2:25: 'I will repay you for the years that the swarming locust has eaten.' The word repay is translated in the King James Version as 'restore'. It means to be made whole again. Isaiah 51:3: 'The Lord will comfort Zion; he will comfort all her waste places, and will make her wilderness like Eden, her desert like the garden of the Lord; joy and gladness will be found in her.'

What an awesome promise. Yet to be fulfilled, it is guaranteed by the faithfulness of God to His Word. Does that have any meaning for a person's life today?

Whether we became a Christian at a young age or much later we know our lives have been plagued at times by moral and spiritual locusts. These may have invaded our lives through our rebellious nature, from being trapped by fifty shades of lust, or due to outside forces. Life had lost its freshness, beauty, purpose and joy. In the years which may remain to us is there any chance of being renewed?

This is the wonderful promise of God. What is beyond our ability to achieve the Lord will do by His grace! What He requires of us is our permission. That means we give Him the right to take control of and nourish our lives. He will do this by His Spirit and Word. Hosea 10:12: 'Sow for yourselves righteousness; break up the fallow ground; for it is time to seek the Lord, that he may come and rain righteousness upon you.' The Lord's mercy provides forgiveness for our wasted years. His persistence with us and discipline allows the Holy Spirit to plough our inner lives and reseed them with holiness, truth, purpose, gratitude and hope.

Over the years I have witnessed the transforming power of God in the lives of young and old. In college I shared time with a couple of soldiers who had seen life in its rawness. Because of their faith, they now had compassion for their previous foes. Watching a once persistent drunk becoming a man of integrity and a supporter of the youth remains vivid in my mind. It is exciting to see a converted prostitute's life remade, then witness her choosing to work for the welfare of those still in the profession. These are but snippets of what the Lord has done, is doing and will continue to do to victims of 'the locust plague'.

We are never immunised from a possible locust swarm. There is an attitude within all of us which attracts these creeping insects. We breed them in the hot houses of worldliness. The Lord may use them as instruments of judgement or warnings that come as a result of our choices. Our protection against creating any sort of breeding program which wastes our moral and spiritual life is not erecting 'hot houses of worldliness'. Titus 2:11-12: 'For the grace of God has appeared bringing salvation to all, training us to renounce impiety and worldly passions, and in the present age to live lives that are self-controlled, upright, and godly.'

Ageless: 'His divine power has given us everything needed for life and godliness, through the knowledge of him who called us by his own glory and goodness. Thus he has given us, through these things, his precious and very great promises, so that through them you may escape from the corruption that is in the world through lust, and may become participants of the divine nature.' 2 Peter 1:3-4.

Leave the Baggage Behind
Day 19

Reading: Philippians 3:1–11

Where was he? It was the time for his recognition as the first king of Israel, but he couldn't be seen. A search was made and Saul from the tribe of Benjamin was found. He had hidden himself among the baggage. (1 Samuel 10:22). Unfortunately, as you read his story, this man with so much potential never freed himself from his 'baggage'.

When we become Christians we enter into this new realm with a lot of our own 'baggage'. Behavioural patterns unfitting for a follower of the Lord and emotional traumas caused by the way others treated us can fill our lives. Then there may be various teachings about life and God which are harmful and untrue. The Lord Jesus Christ knows such baggage can be an excuse not to rise up and fulfil our calling. It also means the joy of the Christian life is squashed under the weight.

Jesus calls us into a relationship of faith in which we can know freedom from such baggage. How does He manage to do that in our lives? John 8:31-32:'If you continue in my word, you are truly my disciples; and you will know the truth, and the truth will make you free.' Free from what? Free to be what? It all hinges on knowing the word Christ spoke about and applying its truth to our lives. Truth is the great 'unwanted baggage' remover.

Baggage is personal and diverse. Therefore, we have to deal with it personally and in the grace and power of the Lord Jesus. This requires us to face up to the issues as we recognise them. Unless we do this they remain excuses for our unwillingness to serve and worship our Saviour. Let us consider three types of 'stuff' people carry around.

The Bible is a book defining acceptable and unacceptable behaviour. It deals with the mind, emotions and their physical expressions. The non-Christian worldview doesn't worry about these things. Once we are converted from that realm we realise that we must have stunk in the nostrils of God. God's response, 1 Corinthians 6:9,11: 'Do you not know that wrongdoers will not inherit the Kingdom of God? ... And this is what you used to be. But you were washed, you were sanctified, you were justified in the name of the Lord Jesus Christ and in the Spirit of our God.' You are free from that worldview. You are free from its condemnation.

Some of you may have been traumatised by the unseen and deadly emotional abuse of others. Nightmares and self-loathing may burden you daily. A sense of unworthiness may enslave your heart. Is the Lord God Almighty able to draw such baggage out of your 'storeroom'? Call to mind the work of Jesus on the cross. Hebrews 9:14: 'The blood of Christ, who through the eternal Spirit offered himself without blemish to God, purify our conscience from dead works to worship the living God.' Let God's word loose upon such rubbish. When the ghosts of the past intrude into the mind confront them with God's word. You are His! You are now the son or daughter of the Most High God. You are precious. You are free!

A person coming out of a cult and into the saving life of Christ can find it difficult to adjust. False teaching tries to rebuild barriers. These are only demolished by the ever living and powerful word of God. If anyone says it is easy to overthrow the past that would indicate they haven't tried. Hold onto the fact that you have been redeemed by Christ from your former life. Then allow His word, His Spirit, His worship to dominate your heart, mind and behaviour. As this takes place, the memory of the forgiven and removed baggage evaporates. You are free!

Ageless: 'How can young people (*including us*) keep their way pure? By guarding it according to your word. With my whole heart I seek you; do not let me stray from your commandments. I treasure your word in my heart, so that I may not sin against you.' Psalm 119:9–11.

Make their Rising Worthwhile
Day 20

Reading: Leviticus 19:32

When I was a child, a long time ago, it was the custom to stand up when an older person entered the room. A similar thing happened on public transport when a senior person or a woman came aboard. This seemed a right and proper thing to do. Little did I or many others realise it had a Biblical mandate. Leviticus 19:32: 'You shall rise before the aged, and defer to the old; and you shall fear your God.'

Cultural norms of the Middle East are reflected in this verse. The aged are honoured, even if they are not liked. Our Western society has displaced this attitude and made youth its centrefold. Perhaps it is the fast pace of our living that has created this loss of respect for older people. I think the spiritual apathy and Biblical ignorance of recent generations also plays a part.

A young person may well ask, 'Why should I rise to my feet simply because an old man or woman enters my space?' A reasonable question, no doubt. If it isn't due to culture surely it comes down to respect, admiration or the position the person holds. Maybe the older person needs to reflect upon why a younger person would count it an honour to stand and greet them.

Within Scripture the term 'elder' is used. Most of the time we understand it to be a position held. However, the word implies grey headedness. The old men (usually) formed a qualified leadership of clan, tribe or nation, along with others such as kings and priests. I like the qualifications listed by the apostle Paul for these men. Consider the following from 1 Titus 1:5-9: 'blameless, God's steward, not arrogant or quick–tempered, not addicted to wine, nor violent or greedy, but hospitable lover of goodness, prudent, upright, devout and self–controlled with a firm grasp of God's Word.'

Can you gain a picture of God's gentleman? He has been proven, not only in the faith, but also the faith has been tested in his life. All of us should be willing to rise and acknowledge such a person. They deserve our respect.

Every believer, especially young men, should aspire to attain such a standing. The saying remains true: 'to be a success in old age you need to start young'.

When Paul wrote to Timothy he shared words all young men, including ministers, need to heed. 1Timothy 5:1: 'Do not speak harshly to an older man, but speak to him as to a father.' To the men who hold leadership positions within the Christian fellowship Timothy is told, 'Let the elders who rule be considered worthy of double honour, especially those who labour in preaching and teaching.' (1 Timothy 5:17). One of the reasons underlying this is found in Hebrews 13:17. Such men have to give an account of their watching over you before the Lord God.

The years can have a negative impact upon the mind, heart and bearing of a person. We have all met the proverbial 'grumpy old men' who imagine they have a right to that title. Unfortunately, people shy away from them for attitudes like that can be debilitating to their own spirit. To meet these people in the Church scene is doubly unpleasant. The Lord's desire is to make such grumpy–ness unnecessary. Christ Jesus wants to deliver them from their bitterness, regret, anger or disappointment. He wants to make all things new and then use personal past experiences as a demonstration of Him making a person whole. We who know such people are called upon to respect them, understand them and try to honour them as the Lord commands. We should also pray for their transformation.

Ageless: To enjoy the privilege inherent in dynamic ageing there are certain requirements. In the words of Paul to Titus, we should determine on pursuing the qualities of temperance, seriousness, prudence, soundness in faith, love and endurance. Who wouldn't stand and defer to such a person with a desire to follow his or her example?

Medicine for a Heavy Heart
Day 21

Reading: Psalm 42

Weight has become an obsession in the Western world. Obesity can cut a person's life short by years. However, is there a way to gauge the load on a person's heart? As we age our hearts and minds accumulate many emotions, memories, nightmares and anxieties. The happy and lovely times seem to float over the heart. On the other hand worries, fears and sorrow become lead weights. Proverbs 15:13: 'A glad heart makes a cheerful countenance, but by sorrow of heart the spirit is broken.'

The Bible poses a hypothetical question in Isaiah 40:12: 'Who has measured the waters in the hollow of his hand and marked off the heavens with a span, enclosed the dust of the earth in a measure, and weighed the mountains in scales and the hills in a balance.' The answer, of course, is the Lord God! He who searches our hearts also knows the burdens it bears.

What can He do to remove some and lighten all other burdens? What has He done to give our hearts strength to carry the load? Two options rise up for consideration. One offers short term relief and the other a more lasting solution. Both wear the imprimatur of heaven. Let's look at the short term relief package. The writers of Proverbs recommended the following wise advice in Proverbs 12:25: 'Anxiety weighs down the human heart, but a good word cheers it up.' Have you had the privilege of saying a healing word to a trouble heart? Words backed up by some positive action including maybe a hug or handshake reach deep within.

Proverbs 17:22a: 'A cheerful heart is a good medicine'. Who can administer it to the person whose spirit has been torpedoed by grief? Laughter, music and pleasant interludes can siphon the sorrow at least for the moment. Add to this Proverbs 27:9: 'Perfume and incense make the heart glad'. The real problem, however, still remains. Cheerfulness drains away. Perfume and incense evaporate. The burdens are lifted for a short spell and that is beneficial. Sometimes they may crash back down again onto the heart.

The need is for a more permanent solution. We seek for a place to cast our burdens. We long for added strength to sustain us. If we are to enjoy dynamic ageing we must know the answers to these questions.

Scripture assures us that the Living Creator God it introduces us to understands our situation. He sees the heart. He knows our histories. He not only empathises with us, our Lord wants to take the load. He is the burden bearer, but only if we do what the psalmist advises. Psalm 55:22: 'Cast your burdens on the Lord, and he will sustain you; he will never permit the righteous to be moved.'

How can we throw an unbearable load onto the invisible Lord? With the spiritual energy of faith taking the Lord Jesus at His word! As we pour out our complaint to Him, confess the angst of our soul and share our sorrows honestly, the heart senses freedom. Beware, however, of the soul's tendency to have some 'elastic' wrapped around some issues. You must cut the cord. That might be through forgiveness, admission or surrender. God will then be able to take the load.

The next matter is drawing in the strength required to sustain our light-heartedness. Jeremiah 15:16: 'Your words were found, and I ate them, and your words became to me a joy and the delight of my heart; for I called upon you name, O Lord, God of hosts.' When Jeremiah said this he was heavy hearted. In sharing his heart with the Lord, Jeremiah found the Lord's dynamic grace.

Ageless: 'You show me the path of life. In your presence there is fullness of joy; in your right hand are pleasures forevermore.' Psalm 16:11.

Escapees from the Old Age Prison
Day 22

Reading: Isaiah 61:1-3

Age for many is a form of prison. The encroaching years restrict freedom of movement, agility, participation and thereby enjoyment. Futility mixed with frustration creates bad cellmates. Each day can witness scenes of men and women 'head-butting' their invisible prison walls. Such self-harm is a sadness all can see, even if they don't understand it.

Do we really believe what Jesus said involved His ministry? In Luke 4:18 he said: 'The Spirit of the Lord is upon me ... to proclaim release to the captives and recovery of sight to the blind, to let the oppressed go free.' What prisons? There are many and they vary. For our purpose we major on the prison we sense our ageing has created. Our Lord doesn't reverse our ageing. He does, however, show us the freedom and scope of trusting in Him. Jesus has the grace to make us content. With this new outlook we can roam the world, yet never leave our room. Our limitations can be turned into prayer grounds for those in the battlefields for Truth.

The Apostle Paul was the Master's restless missionary. He always wanted to go to the regions not yet touched by the Gospel. How frustrating it must have been for him to spend so much time in prisons. How can Paul's attitude help us deal with our prison like situations? Philippians 4:11-12: 'I have learned to be content with whatever I have. I know what it is to have little, and I know what it is to have plenty. In any and all circumstances I have learned the secret of being well-fed and of going hungry, of having plenty and of being in need.'

I appreciate his use of the word 'learned'! To me it implies he had to wrestle with his nature and circumstance, his passion to serve and the limitations of his situation. This will be our lot also. May we plead with the Lord to give us a teachable spirit!

Paul and Silas's time in the Philippians' prison worked out for the salvation of the jail warder and his family. It also confronted the town officials with their injustices to these missionaries. Look at their time in the Caesarean prison. He was locked up for two years. He could have gone stir crazy. However, the Lord brought Roman governors plus King Agrippa and his wife Bernice to hear his testimony. I wonder also how many criminals and prison warders Paul was able to speak to in that time?

Can you sense the Lord inviting you to consider what He can do in what, for you, is a prison? Often God has placed one of his sick and fragile saints beside a sufferer in hospital. From their weakness they have shared faith and hope with another. There is medicine to the soul which takes place when a crippled believer writes to encourage a servant of God in a pagan society.

For me the most thrilling part of Paul's times in the prison of Rome embraces two facets. One, of course, has to be his letter writing. Men and women pour over these most of their lives and are constantly blessed, challenged and renewed in faith and hope. The other aspect is Paul's unquenchable desire to introduce people to Jesus. In some of his letters Paul mentions Onesimus. He was a runaway slave who had forfeited his life. This slave gave his life to Christ and was to be sent back to his owner, Philemon. This man was a disciple of Christ, and on that basis the apostle pleads for Onesimus. Paul's letter to the slave owner is beautiful.

When our hearts throb with conviction about the goodness and grace of the Lord Jesus Christ no prison will restrain it. We may not be as forthright as Paul, yet by the power of the Holy Spirit, we can make our 'prisons' lighthouses of hope.

Ageless: 'I am the Lord; I have called you in righteousness, I have taken you by the hand and kept you; I have given you as a covenant to the people, a light to the nations, to open the eyes of the blind, to bring out the prisoners from the dungeon, from the prison those who sit in darkness.' Isaiah 42:6-7.

Where Dynamic Ageing Begins
Day 23

Reading: John 10:1–10

Dynamic ageing is about meaning, not muscle. It can be possessed by the weak and the invalid, yet missed by the strong and healthy. Dynamic ageing requires living in a spiritual dimension rather than being hypnotised by the secular. The dynamics for all of this begins on a battlefield.

In the book of Amos we read about God's ultimatum to Israel. The nation was intent on doing its own thing. This was even in the face of the Lord God's discipline. His words to the nation are applicable to everyone at a certain point in time. Amos 4:12: 'Therefore thus I will do to you, O Israel; because I will do this to you, prepare to meet your God, O Israel.'

God called upon the people to engage in an act of war, a contest of strength and will to gain control. Who will be Sovereign? Such a contest appears uneven and stupid. However, within the spiritual realm it is fought out everyday by someone, somewhere. Can you remember when you thought about taking God on when He asked you to let Him be your Sovereign?

The weapons at our disposal to defeat His right to our lives are the following:

(A) personal righteousness

(B) all religions lead to Heaven

(C) the pleading of ignorance.

What is the weapon the Lord raises against us? His Word! Hebrews 4:12-13: 'Indeed, the word of God is living and active, sharper than any two-edged sword, piercing until it divides soul from spirit, joints from marrow; it is able to judge the thoughts and intents of the heart. And before him no creature is hidden, but all are naked and laid bare to the eyes of the one to whom we must render an account.' If we can prove our weapons are stronger and more effective we win

We know our goodness will not stand before the holiness required by the Lord. If everyone falls short of their own standard, what hope do they have when measured by God's? One strike and you are out. How many strikes do you imagine are against you? (A) is answered!

We may not like what Jesus said in John 14:6, but it is either true or false. Who would dare make Jesus out to be a liar when He said, 'I am the way, and the truth, and the life. No one comes to the Father except through me.' (B) is answered!

Pleading ignorance is never an excuse. It's a person's responsibility to seek out the truth and accept it. Jeremiah 29:13: 'When you search for me, you will find me; if you seek me with all your heart.' (C) is answered!

The trouble is the Bible remains unbreakable. More than that, our moral and religious armour melts when we wave the Scriptures across them! Then we realise our nakedness. We are defenceless. What are our options? Run! But where can we hide? Surrender! Dynamic ageing can begin at that point in time. We kneel in submission. Our Lord and Sovereign, Jesus, lifts us up and calls us conquerors. 2 Chronicles 30:8: 'Do not be stiffed-necked as your ancestors were, but yield yourselves to the Lord and come to his sanctuary, which he has sanctified for ever, and serve the Lord your God, so that his fierce anger may turn away from you.'

We engage in a self-justifying war without any possible victory when we take up our weapons against God. Remember, God has the last word. Will it be 'Depart into outer darkness'? Or will it be 'Come into the joy of the Lord'? The joy comes when by faith we make Jesus Christ our sovereign Lord and Saviour. A new, dynamic, eternal and challenging life begins.

Ageless: 'No longer present your members to sin as instruments of wickedness, but present yourselves to God as those who have been brought from death to life, and present your members to God as instruments of righteousness.' (Romans 6:13)

Songs in the Night
Day 24

Reading: Psalm 77:1-14

'And it was night!'

The words emphasising the physical and spiritual environment surrounding Judas's betrayal of Jesus. They add a deeper, darker dimension than if the scenario had been in daylight. When those words are added to our experiences, we also know a deeper pain and fear than in the night than we felt in the day. Storms feel more ferocious, loneliness is sensed more keenly and shame haunts more eerily in the dark.

Christ Jesus felt the assaulting power of the darkest of nights. He knew it was coming. He accepted it as part of the Father's plan to weave it into our salvation. What is recorded about the way Jesus handled the encroaching night? He joined with His disciples after the Passover to sing a hymn (probably part or whole of Psalm 118). Then together, they went to the Mount of Olives, where Jesus overcame the night through prayer.

In our ageing the nights can be long, tedious, uncomfortable and haunting. The psalmist recounted his experience in Psalm 77:4-6: 'You keep my eyelids from closing; I am so troubled that I cannot speak. I consider the days of old, and remember the years of long ago. I commune with my heart in the night; I meditate and search my spirit.' (The King James Version says in part: 'I call to remembrance my song in the night'). Is there in that thought something more therapeutic than a pill?

What song in the night would he compose or recite? What would we do if we had the ability? I think there is a clue at least to the themes he and we could use in Psalm 119:54-55: 'Your statutes have been my songs wherever I make my home. I remember your name in the night, O Lord, and keep your law.' For our mouths to sing, shout or simply say something we have composed on a theme from the Bible means we know it.

Faith and knowledge are necessary for us to write a personal song from a godly encounter. What is required for us to hear the song God wants to sing to us in our night times? Ears that hear and a will which obeys the word of the Lord! Psalm 42:8: 'By day the Lord commands his steadfast love, and at night his song is with me …'

Scripture tells of a terrible time yet to come. Across the centuries some of Christ's servants have felt its unpleasant and powerful shadow. When the full force of the 'night' falls the followers of Christ Jesus will do it tough. They'll find serving Him will be a capital offence. Jesus put it this way in John 9:4: 'We must work the works of him who sent me while it is day; night is coming when no one can work.' Such a period precedes the return of the Lord whose coming will be in wrath and holy judgement.

The outcome of Jesus Christ's return is beautifully, majestically spelt out in Zephaniah 3:17. Remember, this follows on from the World's darkest 'night'. 'The Lord, your God, is in your midst, a warrior who gives victory; he will rejoice over you with gladness, he will renew you in his love; he will exult over you with loud singing as on a day of festival.' There will never be the darkness of such a night again. What is the people's response? Zephaniah 3:14: 'Sing aloud, O daughter of Zion, shout, O Israel! Rejoice and exult with all your heart …'

The songs we compose or recite during our nights will one day give way to songs of praise, joy and victory. By faith, we rehearse them now, even as we shed tears or our voices quiver. May we sing our song to the Lord with a grateful heart. May we hear Him sing to us in our spirit through a faithful heart.

No more night!

Ageless: 'So the ransomed of the Lord shall return, and come to Zion with singing; everlasting joy shall be upon their heads; and they shall obtain joy and gladness, and sorrow and sighing shall flee away.' Isaiah 51:11.

Be a Spiritual (Grand) Mother
Day 25

Reading: Titus 2:3-5

Mary married a minister. What was expected of a minister's wife? Mary hadn't been given instructions on it, even though she had been to a Bible college. She was fortunate to be taken under the wing of some of the older ministers' wives. They helped her in the transition period from student, to wife and a minister's wife. These women were dynamic role models for Mary and many others.

Titus was commissioned to establish a doctrinally sound church which would express itself in worthy behaviour and godly relationships. Five specific groups are mentioned in the letter. They were the aged men and women, younger women and men plus slaves. Titus 2:1: 'As for you, teach what is consistent with sound doctrine.' Why? Paul wrote in Titus 3:8: 'I desire that you insist on these things (*previous verses*) so that those who have come to believe in God may be careful to devote themselves to good works; these things are excellent and profitable to everyone.'

How would you as a young man, probably single, feel about instructing the older women on showing the Christian lifestyle? More than that, to encourage them to be examples and teachers of the younger women in being Christian wives? Did Titus hear what Paul told Timothy, who was to be involved with similar situations? Timothy was told to treat the older women as mothers. These older women were to seize their situation as an opportunity to honour the Lord. This ministry was to bless the younger women and thereby, enrich the fabric of the Church's life. Dare I add that by such a ministry the community's life would also feel the change!

Unfortunately, not all aged women are worthy role models or fit for the Lord's service. However, if they had a heart to learn and a will to measure up what an inspiration they would be! Paul makes a short list of the basics on which to build an effective arena of service. Three out of the four stipulations deal with their personal demeanour. It is taken for granted they had a testimony in their salvation. Have you ever shared your conversion with others? It may have been person to person or by letter, email or in a magazine, but you need to share your story. However, it is easy to write or speak about your testimony but does your life match your words. Will those who know you give their approval to what you say? That is the emphasis Paul was making. Notice from the reading that these older women needed to have reverent behaviour. How would you define that today? The word points to a lifestyle suitable to a sacred character. It was a description expressing a style of living outwardly associated with God. Matthew 5:16: 'Let your light shine before others, so that they may see your good works and give glory to your Father in heaven.'

The mouth then takes prominence. Be careful what you say about others. Be careful what you put to your lips – and how much. Be careful to teach that which is good. In the world of arranged marriages it becomes evident why Paul insists on teaching how to love the husband and the child. The word for love isn't 'agape' but comes from 'phileo', to love as a friend. How meaningful. This embraces the idea of tenderness, unselfishness and a readiness to serve. Such a love blossoms into the beauty of the deeper, richer, unshakeable love called 'agape'.

The dynamic older women were to teach what is good. That opens up a whole realm for consideration. In the immediate context it zooms into helping the younger women understand the Christian faith through doctrine. Then it must be expressed in their most intimate relationships. This would not be the full stop of the teaching. It was just the beginning. The reason, as Paul put it in Titus 2:5: 'So that the word of God may not be discredited.'

Ageless: 'Hear, my child, your father's instruction, and do not reject your mother's teaching.' Proverbs 1:8.

Total Dynamic Ageing
Day 26

Reading: 1 Thessalonians 5:16-17

(This devotional takes the form of a soliloquy: a person seemingly talking to himself, but conscious that God is being addressed. I trust you will adapt it to yourself.)

Imagine that. Me, set aside for sacred use. Wow! Your word says it covers the total me; body, soul and spirit. Lord, that is beyond my comprehension. As I read the Bible on the subject of my body before Christ and after Christ, I am amazed. You turned the habitation of self indulgence and ungodly expression into your dwelling place. Your power and grace turned a slum into a temple. Thanks!

I noticed also, Lord, you never speak about the condition of the body. It may be fit or twisted, whole or with parts missing, youthful or wrinkled with age, yet you make it your abiding place. Christ Jesus, you are so wonderful to us. I must admit, however, I'm looking forward to the time you lift me and others up into your presence. There we will have a new and glorified body.

Can I be honest and open with you, Lord? When I asked you to be my Lord and Saviour I didn't really think I needed such a major overhaul. I considered my soul to be reasonably acceptable to you, especially when I compared myself with others. How wrong I was! You knew me better than I knew myself. Jeremiah defined my soul as devious and perverse, and I was offended. Then your Holy Spirit made me stand in your light. You are the unalterable standard for entrance into heaven. My goodness was in tatters.

What you did on the cross at Calvary isn't merely history. It is an eternal 'now'. When your blood flowed, your life shed, it became my opportunity to be forgiven, cleansed and set apart for yourself. Somehow, Lord Jesus, you reached into my inner being and removed the resident spiritual principle called 'the body of sin' (Romans 6:6). I now understand I could never enter heaven with that thing dominating my nature. Across the years, you have shown me that the nature of my soul is still self-obsessed. Fortunately for me, your Spirit uses your word as a scalpel to cut and as a balm to heal.

Isn't it strange how people like me know about God yet never really know Him until we believe in you. To all intents and purposes I was dead to you and you were merely an idea to me. Then the gospel came knocking on my mind and captured my heart. What a momentous night it was when I surrendered my will to you by faith. You gave my spirit life. I am now able to know you, have fellowship with you, to worship and serve you. Life has never been so meaningful, so alive and hopeful.

As I get older I want to express my gratitude to you for what you have done in and with me. I hope that my ageing will be dynamic in your sight. My body may be wearing out and my soul not as sharp as other folks, but I praise you Lord for my spirit, which seems to be constantly refreshed by yours. So it is, Lord, I would like Paul's words to the Thessalonians to be active in my life.

Set me apart for your use in my everyday experiences. Even if I become bedridden, feeble or forgetful, I want your fragrance to reach through me and bless others. I cannot manufacture this. You must always be the source and the strength. I want you to receive the glory. For me, in sickness or health, in good times or tough ones, I want to know dynamic ageing.

Ageless: 'We do not lose heart. Even though our outer nature is wasting away, our inner nature is being renewed day by day.' 2 Corinthians 4:16

Keeping the Spiritual Weeds under Control
Day 27

Reading: Proverbs 24:30-34

We are encouraged to plan for our retirement. This usually centres around financial matters and becoming one of the 'grey nomads'. It's vitally important. To neglect these matters can sour what should be a most interesting time. One part most often neglected when leaving the work scene is our spiritual life. Do we make arrangements for enriching and expanding it or are we happy to maintain the status quo?

Living in an area where many of the people are retired, I've noticed how easily spiritual weeds overrun the flowers of Christian commitment. Lovely people with a faith in Jesus Christ often move to a new area. Unfortunately, church involvement becomes a convenience rather than a commitment. How quickly the thorns, thistles and briers of Proverbs can begin growing in the soul.

'The way of the lazy is overgrown with thorns ...' (Proverbs 15:19). Many an attractive weed has irritating thorns. There are many fun activities and appealing pastimes waiting to divert a disciple of Christ from fully–fledged devotion. The person may not be idle in the physical and social sense, but he or she can still be neglectful of the spiritual. The result? Spiritual thorns. Applying another picture from Proverbs 19:15 to the spiritual realm will reveal a twofold effect: 'Laziness brings on deep sleep; an idle person will suffer hunger.' How would you interpret 'sleep' and 'hunger' in the Christian life?

Dynamic ageing requires constant attention. There is a continual need to eject thorns, thistle and briers. The encouragement for this comes from Hebrews 6:10-12: 'God is not unjust; he will not overlook your work and the love that you showed for his sake in serving the saints, as you still do. And we want each of you to show the same diligence so as to realise the full assurance of hope to the very end, so that you may not become sluggish, but imitators of those who through faith and patience inherit the promises.'

Did you pick up a key word in the above verses? The opposite to being diverted from our commitment or lazy in our faith is to be diligent. The Scriptures are saturated with calls to be alert, watchful, on guard, attentive, striving. To me, that is a sign that the soul has a tendency to be seduced by the charms of the world or smothered by the weeds of neglect.

'The appetite of the lazy craves, and gets nothing, while the appetite of the diligent is richly supplied.' (Proverbs 13:4). The Lord doesn't wait on those who merely are wanting but not actively pursuing the spiritual life. He does provide for the genuine searcher from His resources. A person may realise his spiritual hunger but is unwilling to expend the energy to satisfy it. Weeds do not nourish, and some will poison body, soul and spirit. The desire of the diligent is to be well nourished by the one called 'the Bread of Life.'. This means when they are called into the presence of their Lord they will be spiritually fit, healthy and vibrant. Few and small will be the weeds that endeavour to gain mastery in such a believer.

In Deuteronomy Moses speaks plainly to the nation as it prepares to enter the Promised Land. The Lord's servant knew the heart of the people and their tendencies for weeds. He tells them in chapter 4:9: 'Take care and watch yourselves closely, so as neither to forget the things that your eyes have seen nor let them slip from your mind all the days of your life; make them known to your children and your children's children.'

Ageless: 'Instead of the thorn shall come up the cypress; instead of the brier shall come up the myrtle; and it shall be to the Lord a memorial, for an everlasting sign that shall not be cut off.' Isaiah 55:13. (The word of the Lord will produce that in the heart of the diligent).

The Dreamtime Cometh
Day 28

Reading: Joel 2:25-32

There are books galore about the meaning of dreams. Some have the wisp of the Christian faith, but most do not. The writer of Ecclesiastes makes two valid comments about dreams. Remember, he is battling spiritual lethargy due to a life of extravagance. What he says does have credibility. Ecclesiastes 5:3, 7: 'Dreams come with many cares ... With many dreams comes vanities and a multitude of words, but fear God'.

With that warning still flashing in the mind remember God has done, is doing and will do his work. Dreams may be part of that to achieve His desire to reach out, to warn, bless and save! How then, are we His ageing citizens of heaven, to understand Joel 2:28: 'Then afterwards I will pour out my spirit on all flesh; your sons and your daughters shall prophesy, your old men shall dream dreams, and your young men shall see visions. Even on the male and female slaves, in those days, I will pour out my spirit.'

Joel sees that, one day, privileges of ministry will be shared between the young and old, the free and the slave. When will this take place? If we take Joel's writing as a guide it happens between the time the Lord takes pity on Israel and the judgement of the nations. This time will be momentous. Read Joel 2:30–3:16.

What can we learn from God's grace in including the ageing believers in what is God's preparation for history's climax? They may not have the drive and energy of the young, but God still values their faithfulness. What I see in the Lord's word to us via Joel is Yahweh's desire for mutual ministry. The young should not feel superior to the aged, the old begrudge the youth, nor men despise the role of women. Together they have a prophetic ministry into a world that is in chaos and descending into judgement.

If you imagine you are having a hard time serving the Lord be encouraged from Joel's writing. The Lord is with His people. The Lord will accomplish

His purposes. The Lord will bless His people. The day of those servants will be harder! What will they need? Faithfulness to God's Spirit, confidence in His word and imaginative methods to reach the nations. Sounds familiar.

Until I began this devotion I admit to not being absorbed in any particular God-given dream. Being in ministry, having a family, praying for people and places, and other matters occupied my waking moments. Now however, I'm asking myself what God given dreams He has in mind for me. What about you? How can I know if they are from Him or my own inclination?

Dreams must be evaluated under the microscope of God's Word. They must be held up to the light of Jesus Christ's character and calling. They must bring honour and glory to our Heavenly Father through our faithfulness. Ezekiel links God's Spirit to the manner of our faith and walk in 36:27: 'I will put my spirit within you, and make you follow my statutes and be careful to observe my ordinances.'

The dreams of the aged may well become the passion of youth to fulfil. We may present the challenge which their enthusiasm and faith will undertake. I'm reminded of David and his son. The King of Israel had the dream and desire to build the temple. The Lord God said 'No!' This man after God's own heart entrusted it to Solomon. The wonderful thing about David was that he prepared the plans, provided much of the money and stirred up support. His dream doesn't bear his name. Who is seen as the builder? Solomon! What can we learn from David's grace?

Ageless: 'There is still a vision for the appointed time; it speaks of the end, and does not lie. If it seems to tarry, wait for it; it will surely come, it will not delay.' Habakkuk 2:3.

Walking by your Heart
Day 29

Reading: Psalm 73

Honest, that's how I would describe the Psalms. They are so transparent in sharing the writer's fears, faith, failures and the fury of foes. Their appeal across the centuries never wanes. They not only speak to us, somehow or other we find ourselves unmasked by similar experiences. Psalm 73 is a psalm has the power to place a mirror before our souls.

The eras are different, but the problem remains the same. The focus of the eyes caused the psalmist's heart to make his walk waver. Psalm 73:2-3: 'As for me, my feet had almost stumbled; my steps had nearly slipped. For I was envious of the arrogant; I saw the prosperity of the wicked.' Have you ever been in that situation?

The inequity of this world is staggering. The psalmist goes on to say that the rich are often careless towards God and of the needs of the suffering. Daily, we hear about corruption in high places and the exploitation of the poor and undernourished. The sense of helplessness which often comes to us as we age can make us fume. Envy can easily rise up in our hearts. When combined with doubt in God's goodness, it can make for a slippery surface for our faith.

As you read the psalm you can sense the rage building up within the writer. Any person with a sense of justice would say 'amen' to Psalm 73:12–14: '… the wicked (*are*) always at ease, they increase in riches. All in vain I have kept my heart clean and washed my hands in innocence. For all day long I have been plagued, and am punished every morning.' Through life's unfairness, many Christians are victims to slippery slopes of doubt, anxiety, a sense of injustice and anger. Knowing this, our Lord and Saviour had already set up a casualty repair centre. But He wants those who have slipped to make their way to it.

Where is it to be found? Psalm 73:16-17: '… it seemed to me a wearisome task, until I went into the sanctuary of God; then I perceived their end.' Was the sanctuary for the psalmist the tabernacle or temple? Unless he was a Levite there was no way for him to get into their area. Did he get as close to it as possible and draw strength from its testimony to God's presence? Did the writer have his own heart space where he communed with the Lord? This would be similar to Jesus when He spoke about going into your room, shutting the door and praying to your Father. Does your heart have its sanctuary where you and your Heavenly Father enjoy each others company?

In the sanctuary of God's word we get the eternal picture. The verdict upon the arrogant and godless is summed up in one of Jesus' parables. Luke 12:20: 'You fool! This very night your life is being demanded of you.'

How can a Christian's willpower maintain his or her spiritual sanity in such an unbalanced world? Ageing doesn't relieve us of our Christian sensitivity and stewardship. We may, however, feel like absconding. What can hold us steady? On what can our eyes focus to strengthen our hearts so we can stay the course? Psalm 94:18-19: 'When I thought "My foot is slipping", your steadfast love, O Lord, held me up. When the cares of my heart are many, your consolations cheer my soul.'

Each of us will know the embarrassment of slipping and being bruised. When it happens to us what do we think God's response is? The psalmist was in no doubt. God still held him and God's counsel would still be available to guide him. He was a bruised believer but still loved. That's grace!

Ageless: 'My flesh and my heart may fail, but God is the strength of my heart and my portion forever.' Psalm 73:26.

The Might of Widows
Day 30

Reading: Luke 21:1-4

Across my ministries I've been amazed and humbled by the faithfulness of widows to the cause of Christ Jesus. They have come in all shapes and sizes and span many years. All their contribution to the life of the local church and its mission is known only to the Lord. I've stood in awe at some of the work these ladies have done to raise money for mission. I've been humbled as I've listened to their prayers, which stretched from the local to the global.

Within the Biblical narrative nine widows are mentioned. For this meditation I've picked three to highlight. Each expressed, in their own ways, a dynamic feature that Yahweh considered important. He wanted future generations to recognise and honour their faithfulness. It seems to me they epitomise why the Lord God has a special affection for these women.

Luke and Mark record Jesus watching a 'poor widow' putting money into the temple treasury. Everyone else, apparently, was lauding the rich as they gave their gifts out of their abundance. Jesus spotted the widow unobtrusively depositing her two copper coins. Was she shy, embarrassed at the paucity of her gift, or simply doing it quietly as unto the Lord? Her two coins were of more worth to God than the abundance of the rich. As Jesus said elsewhere 'they have their reward' from the people's applause!

Motives are only fully known by the Lord. He knew her heart and its devotion to her heavenly Father. Jesus, by highlighting her gift, has given us an example of dynamic devotion. How did God's grace meet her in her poverty? We will never know, but we rest in the knowledge that it would have been sufficient for her.

Another widow plays a small but important role in the birth narrative of Jesus. Anna's prophet husband died after only seven years of marriage. She was now eighty-four years old. Was she bitter? Did she blame God for such a thing? Did she drop out of worship? Definitely not! Anna had devoted herself to worship and service of the Lord at the temple. What a thrill it must have been to have been given a 'God opportunity' to meet the Baby. She perceived Him to be the promised Messiah (Luke 2:36-38).

Many Christian fellowships and organisations have experienced the faithfulness of women and widows such as Anna. To be in their company when the Lord God presents Himself to them in some form of 'a God moment' is a joy to behold. Worship of such quality as Anna's is its own blessing. However, it can take on a dynamic power of its own when the opportunity arises.

The third widow comes from outside Israel. Jesus Christ uses an encounter recorded in 1Kings 17 to highlight the Father's wide ranging mercy and providence (Luke 4:25-26). It centres around the prophet Elijah. He needed a safe place to hide from the threat of death. Queen Jezebel had decreed a bounty on his head against him. Had the Lord prepared a rich man for such an honour? No! It was a widow and her only son who lived in Zarephath in Sidon.

Why? To bless the woman and display His providential grace. When Elijah appeared at her door he claimed Middle Eastern hospitality's rule! She was not only poor, she was preparing their final meal before starvation beset them. The whole land was in a dreadful famine. However, this Gentile woman shared her meagre rations with him. Through Elijah, the Lord worked His miracle of providence and the meagre rations didn't run out until after the famine ceased.

The widow of Zarephath expresses to me the dynamic generosity of the poor even when it leads to their own hurt. This is often the story from those who have tasted it in long or short term mission work. Also, I believe the Lord has recorded it to highlight the need for us to be 'Elijah' to such hospitable people. This is an act of gratitude to a dynamic act of hospitality. Both are pleasing to the Lord.

Ageless: Hebrews 13:2: 'Do not neglect to show hospitality to strangers, for by doing that some have entertained angels without knowing it.' I might add that, through such strangers, God has some surprises for you.

It's Departure Time
Day 31

Reading: 2 Timothy 4:1-8

In the Wild West stories I've read there is a recurring phrase: 'They died with their boots on'. I imagine that is where the term 'Boot Hill' comes from. When I read the story of the early apostles and many since, another phrase could be coined: 'They died with the sandals of the Gospel of peace still on' (Ephesians 6:15).

As Christians we know our destination, but we don't know our departure time. We are told to 'be ready'. How? By being properly dressed for travel! What does that involve? From our perspective it means fulfilling our calling, celebrating our Lord through worship. It also means not thinking old age means taking off our 'sandals'!

There's a lot of truth in the saying, 'it's not how you begin the race but how you finish.' Most of us can look back and shudder at our early faith and obedience endeavours. I do, but am comforted by the sheer grace and patience of our God. His mercy became 'fuel' for my growth in understanding His word. It also meant having the strength to handle the burdens imposed on me.

In the Old Testament there is a statement by Jacob as he was dying: 'I am about to be gathered to my people' (Genesis 49:29). It had the sense of homecoming. Jesus further explained it in Matthew 22:32, 'Have you not read what was said to you by God, I am the God of Abraham, the God of Isaac and the God of Jacob? He is God not of the dead, but of the living.' Later in John 14, the Lord Jesus enlarged upon Jacob's statement. The Lord widened the sense of 'homecoming' to include all who have made Him Lord and Saviour.

Christ Jesus' resurrection has robbed Death of its dread. It is still the last enemy, but it is without the spirit-crushing power of condemnation before the Holy God. That is, if you belong to Jesus through your commitment by faith! 1 John 5:11-12: 'This is the testimony: God gave us eternal life, and this life is in his Son. Whoever has the Son has life; whoever does not have the Son of God does not have life.'

Paul was one of those who knew his departure date. Caesar had condemned him to death by a sword thrust to the neck. The words Paul wrote to Timothy reveal how firmly the Gospel sandals were tied to his feet. From his Roman cell he encouraged Timothy to continue to preach the word and endure hardship for Christ's name. Then, before final greetings, he talks about being ready to go.

For him, martyrdom was an offering unto the Lord Jesus. The battle cry of the kingdom of God is 'Jesus is Lord.' It confronted the claim of this world's kingdoms. Jesus alone is Lord, worthy of worship and He is the coming King. It is the martyrs' testimony in death. It is to be our boast in life. It is our conviction as we finish our race of life. Therefore, whenever His servants depart, there is a sense of destiny and victory.

Paul's use of 'drink–offering' points to the Mosaic ritual which came at the end of the animal sacrifice (Numbers 15:1-10). It signified the giving by the worshipper of something personal and for God's use alone. Paul likened his death to it. Here was the culmination of his life, which is best described as a living sacrifice (Romans 12:1) being poured out. It represented a free-will offering, a pleasant fragrance to the Lord.

My daughter, many years ago, gave me a small cloth poster. The words said: 'Life is not measured by length but by its depth'. We who have been granted long life in the company of Christ should also be out in the deep, treading the waters of faith and service. Onlookers might think we are foolish and alone. What they don't know is that the Lord is treading water with us and holding us up.

To be honest I'm not enthusiastic about dying. I am, however, excited by what it leads to! Let Paul express it for me: 'I have fought the good fight, I have finished the race, I have kept the faith. From now on there is reserved for me the crown of righteousness, which the Lord, the righteous judge, will give me on that day, and not only to me but also to all who long for his appearing.' (2 Timothy 4:8).

Ageless: 'This grace was given to us in Christ Jesus before the ages began, but it has now been revealed through the appearing of our Saviour Christ Jesus, who abolished death and brought life and immortality to light through the gospel.' (2 Timothy 1:9-10).

Mirror on the Wall

The mirror on the wall doesn't lie

What it sees I cannot deny

Hair is greying, retreating

Shoulders once square, drooping

Eyes and sound are dimming

The back is bent

Energy spent

Life's race

A walk

The mirror on the wall doesn't lie

It reveals my outer history

But cannot see my destiny!

The mirror of God's word doesn't lie

What it says I'll not deny

Grey hair is an honour

Grace inner strength renewing

Eyes, ears by faith beholding

A new creation

Mercy beckons

Life's race

To run.

The mirror of God's word doesn't lie

It reveals my inner history

And affirms my destiny!

The mirror on the wall doesn't lie

It reveals my frailty in ageing.

The mirror of God's word doesn't lie

It proclaims my eternity.

One makes me anaemic

The other says I'm dynamic!

I'll not deny the mirror on the wall

It shows me my mortality.

I'll affirm God's mirror in my heart

It points to my eternity!

Insights to Share

In groups or for personal reflection the following questions are designed to stir the mind, bless the heart and revive the memory.

Down Memory Lane

What board games and sports did you enjoy in your youth?

What did you like most about your life when you were growing up?

Did you go to Sunday school? Where?

Do you have any special memories of anniversaries and picnics?

Can you recall your favourite songs, hymns, choruses, books, movies?

Down Memory Lane 2

Did you go to church as a family?

Do you have any anecdotes from your time in church as a youth?

Did you go to church camps? Where were they held?

Was there any special times in the church's life you recall?

Down Memory Lane 3

Who is your favourite 'oldie' from the Bible? Why?

Who encouraged you the most in your faith?

Can you recall what led you to trust Jesus as your personal Saviour?

Creating a New 'Memory Lane' 4

What mission society or country would you be interested in praying and supporting? Why?

Considering your circumstances how can you exercise a spiritual influence?

How would you explain the difference between merriment and joy?

Did Jesus have a sense of humour? Give some examples.

What worries you about things today? Does the Bible offer answers or hope?

www.ingramcontent.com/pod-product-compliance
Lightning Source LLC
Chambersburg PA
CBHW071029080526
44587CB00015B/2552